LED ZEPPELIN

BY DAVE LEWIS

Copyright © 1994 Omnibus P...

Co...
Pi...

ISBN: 0

Book Sales Limite
Music Sales Corporation, 2...   ...10010, USA.
Music Sales Pty Limited, 30-32 C........ Street, Sydney, Australia, NSW 2000, Australia.

To the Music Trade only:
Music Sales Limited, 8/9, Frith Street, London W1V 5TZ, UK.

Photo credits: Front cover: Aubrey Powell. Richie Aaron/Redferns: 32; Glenn A. Baker Archives/Redferns: 6;
Kevin Cummings: 102; Ian Dickson/Redferns: vi, 59; London Features International: 26, 36, 52, 94;
Michael Putland/Retna: iv, 19, 43, 65, 93; Swansong: 66, 74, 80; Matthew Taylor: 96.
Colour Section: Richie Aaron/Redferns: 4/5, 7, 8t; Ian Dickson/Redferns: 1; LFI: 2, 3, 6, 7r, 8b.

Every effort has been made to trace the copyright holders of the photographs in this book but one or
two were unreachable. We would be grateful if the photographers concerned would contact us.

Printed in the United Kingdom by Ebenezer Baylis & Son Limited, Worcester.

A catalogue record for this book is available from the British Library.

OMNIBUS PRESS
LONDON · NEW YORK · SYDNEY

Led Zeppelin's first photo call, October 1968

CONTENTS

INTRODUCTION v

THE TEN ALBUM LEGACY 1

    LED ZEPPELIN 3

    LED ZEPPELIN II 13

    LED ZEPPELIN III 23

    ✾⚲🎽Ⓟ 31

    HOUSES OF THE HOLY 41

    PHYSICAL GRAFFITI 51

    PRESENCE 63

    SOUNDTRACK FROM THE FILM 'THE SONG REMAINS THE SAME' 71

    IN THROUGH THE OUT DOOR 77

    CODA 85

LED ZEPPELIN REMASTERED 1990 & 1993 91

TRACK INDEX 103

US tour, 1977

iNTRODUCTiON

Led Zeppelin began life as the vehicle for guitarist Jimmy Page to extend the ideals of the disbanding Yardbirds, the pioneer British group whose alumni also included two other outstanding guitarists, Eric Clapton and Jeff Beck. By 1968 The Yardbirds had long since passed the peak of their popularity in the UK, and their hybrid style of pop psychedelia and R&B seemed to find favour only on the then emerging American FM rock radio stations and the US college and ballroom circuit.

Inspired by the chance to pursue a more adventurous and dynamic style with what remained of the group, and with a perceptive eye towards the US market, Page and manager Peter Grant set about re-forming The New Yardbirds in the autumn of 1968. Recruited first was seasoned session arranger/bassist/keyboard player John Paul Jones with whom Page had worked during many recording sessions in the past. In contrast, singer Robert Plant and drummer John Bonham, both from the Midlands, were relatively inexperienced in the ways of the music industry but Page had shrewdly judged their talent and enthusiasm for the project. Together the quartet played out a previously contracted tour of Scandinavia and went into Olympic studios in Barnes to cut their first album.

Rarely has studio time been more economically applied. That album, titled simply 'Led Zeppelin' – The New Yardbirds name was soon ditched – and recorded in a mere 30 hours, laid the foundations for one of the most spectacular careers in rock. The music that Led Zeppelin left behind after 12 years at the top is as influential in the 1990s as it was in the 1970s when they dominated album charts and concert arenas around the world.

What makes Led Zeppelin's ten album catalogue so durable is Page's sense of dynamics and the overall diversity of the music. Most of Led Zeppelin's music was hard rock driven remorselessly by the extraordinary power of John Bonham's drumming, and this would inspire a whole genre that became – with decidedly mixed results – heavy metal. But as Robert Plant found his confidence as a lyricist and John Paul Jones came to the fore as a subtle arranger, Led Zeppelin travelled way beyond that limited genre and were able to bring in an assortment of musical ideas from outside the accepted rock traditions.

Within the Led Zeppelin canon can be found strange Eastern tunings, ethereal folk arrangements, syncopated funk rhythms and jazz improvisations. It was this quest for experimentation within Page's blues rock riffing that has elevated the group's catalogue to a permanent lofty position in the history of 20th century popular music. And it's this catalogue that continues to influence new generations of potential rock heroes, whether it's heavy metallists trying but rarely succeeding to improve on 'Whole Lotta Love', soft rockers who take their cue from the melodious opening bars of 'Stairway To Heaven', heavy bluesers inspired by 'Since I've Been Loving You' or grunge rockers who head into territory already explored by Led Zeppelin in 'Wearing And Tearing'. Sooner or later someone somewhere will develop Led Zeppelin's Eastern leanings in 'Kashmir' or the light and shade acoustic blues of 'Babe, I'm Gonna Leave You', or even the quasi funk of 'The Crunge'.

However familiar you may be with these albums, this guide is designed to enhance the listening experience and take you back to the music with fresh enthusiasm. It was written and researched with my own accustomed ears never far away from the turntable or CD scanner. It is a listening experience now enhanced by Jimmy Page, ever the sonic architect, who with much pride and care has restored Led Zeppelin's music to its best possible resonance with the 'Remasters' series of releases.

Led Zeppelin's catalogue remains a vital kaleidoscope of historic rock music. This close study of every individual track the group recorded will – in the lines of one of their most outstanding compositions – take you there...

Dave Lewis is the editor and publisher of 'Tight But Loose'*, the acclaimed UK Led Zeppelin fanzine, and the author of 'Led Zeppelin: A Celebration' (Omnibus Press, 1991), the definitive reference book on the group. In 1992 he was the co-organiser of the first Led Zeppelin fans' convention in London, and he is widely regarded by fans – and the group themselves – as a foremost authority on Led Zeppelin and their music.*

For details of Dave Lewis' Led Zeppelin Information Service which incorporates the Tight But Loose *magazine, send an sae to TBL, 14 Totnes Close, Bedford MK40 3AX.*

LED ZEPPELIN

LED ZEPPELIN II

LED ZEPPELIN III

HOUSES OF THE HOLY

PHYSICAL GRAFFITI

PRESENCE

THE SONG REMAINS
THE SAME

IN THROUGH THE OUT DOOR

CODA

THE TEN ALBUM LEGACY

A TRACK BY TRACK ANALYSIS OF THE OFFICIAL
LED ZEPPELIN CATALOGUE

Between 1969 and 1982 Led Zeppelin released a total of 10 albums. Since their demise in 1980, sales of those albums have continued to build up, ensuring the group's position as the holders of one of the most buoyant back catalogues in the history of recorded sound. Over the next 112 pages, these 10 albums are dissected and analysed track by track. Each song's origin, its place in their live repertoire, and its overall standing in the Zeppelin catalogue is assessed. The result is an intensive study of the music that can be found within their l0 album legacy. From 'Good Times Bad Times' to 'Wearing And Tearing', this is the definitive study of Led Zeppelin on record.

LED ZEPPELiN

ATLANTIC RECORDS

ORIGINAL ISSUE 588 171, RE-ISSUE K40031

The début Led Zeppelin album is the recorded statement of their first few weeks together. It's also a fair representation of their initial blues / rock stage act that had been tested on Scandinavian audiences just prior to entering Olympic studios in October 1968 to lay down their first studio tracks. The material selected for the album had been well rehearsed and pre-arranged by the four, one of the primary reasons it took only 30 studio hours to complete.

When it came to securing a new deal for the group, Peter Grant negotiated a massive five-album £200,000 package with Jerry Wexler and Ahmet Ertegun of Atlantic Records in New York. This ended speculation that they would extend The Yardbirds' previous association with Epic in America and EMI in the UK. Part of the Atlantic deal allowed Grant and Zeppelin to retain virtually complete control of artistic matters. They also formed their own company, Superhype, to handle all publishing rights. It was also agreed that all Led Zeppelin records would appear on the famous red Atlantic label, as opposed to its less distinguished Atco subsidiary which had been used for Atlantic's non soul or R&B acts in the past. This gave them the distinction of being the first white UK act on the prestigious Atlantic label.

It took a mere 30 hours to record 'Led Zeppelin' in Olympic Studios just south of the River Thames in Barnes in West London. In the hi-tech atmosphere of the Nineties, when groups of far less distinction or pedigree casually spend well over a year (and £200,00) making an album, it seems incongruous that this was all the time it took Jimmy Page and engineer Glyn Johns to produce 'Led Zeppelin I'. But Led Zeppelin (or at least two of them, and manager Peter Grant) were already seasoned studio professionals and since the group didn't have a record contract at the time, Page and Grant were obliged to stump up for the studio time out of their own pockets. Unlike so many of today's profligate 'stars', there was no record company money to waste on excessive studio time; Zeppelin, acting according to an unofficial credo that in time would change the face of the record industry, were self-sufficient every step of the way.

The songs that the group recorded in a period of just nine days at a reputed cost of £1,782 had been well rehearsed and arranged on the Scandinavian tour the four undertook as The New Yardbirds, and 'old' studio hands with the experience of Page and Jones could be relied upon to get maximum value from every hour (and pound) spent at Olympic. With the possible exception of the 12 hours that The Beatles took to record their first album at Abbey Road, rarely has studio time been used so economically. Led Zeppelin's début album went on to gross more than £3.5 million, just short of 20,000 times more than they invested!

The artistic control of their output would extend to their sleeve designs and on the first album, Jimmy chose a simple black on white illustration of the Hindenburg airship going down, as Keith Moon had put it, like a 'Lead' Zeppelin. It was later claimed by The Who's John Entwistle that this sleeve design had been earmarked for the group he, Moon and Page had talked about forming a couple of years earlier. The back cover photo was taken by former Yardbird Chris Dreja, who quit to take up a career in photography during the evolution of The New Yardbirds. During the first few weeks of release in the UK, the sleeve was printed with the name and Atlantic logo in turquoise. This was switched to the common orange print later in the year, creating a much sought after sleeve rarity. The whole design was co-ordinated by George Hardie, with whom they would later work on future sleeves.

Hardie recalls that he originally offered the group a design based on an old club sign in San Francisco – a multi-sequential image of a phallic Zeppelin airship up in the clouds. Jimmy turned down the idea, but it was retained as the logo that adorned the back cover of both the first and second albums and a number of early press advertisements.

The Led Zeppelin album was initially

released in America on January 17, 1969, to capitalise on their first US visit. Before that, Atlantic distributed a few hundred advance white label copies to key radio stations and reviewers. A positive reaction to its contents, coupled with a good reaction to their opening gigs, resulted in the album generating 50,000 advance orders. It entered the *Billboard* chart at number 99. From there it rose to number 40, then 28, reaching the Top 20 and rising as high as number 10. In all it enjoyed 73 weeks on the chart, returning for further spells in 1975 and 1979. In the UK it was issued on March 28. Originally it appeared as Atlantic 588 171 via Polydor's distribution. It was one of a new breed of stereo only releases, as up until 1969 most albums were available as stereo or mono versions. When the Warner group took over the Atlantic catalogue in 1972, the number switched to K40031. On April 12,1969, the Led Zeppelin début album began a 79-week run on the British chart, peaking at number six.

The album was advertised in selected music papers under the slogan 'Led Zeppelin – the only way to fly'. And fly it certainly did. Time has done nothing to diminish the quality of one of the finest début albums ever recorded. There's an urgency and enthusiasm about their performance that retains timeless charm. The nine cuts offer a *tour de force* of powerful yet often subtle dynamics. There are just so many highlights: the spacey blues feel of 'I Can't Quit Baby', the clever light and shade approach on 'Babe I'm Gonna Leave You', Page bowing maniacally on 'Dazed And Confused' and 'How Many More Times', and throughout it all the young Robert Plant lays down a piercing vocal style set to become the group's trademark. And let's not forget the fact that with this album, Page virtually invents the guitar riff as a key songwriting component.

GOOD TIMES BAD TIMES
PAGE, JONES & BONHAM
STUDIO: OLYMPIC STUDIOS, LONDON

At two minutes, 43 seconds, this is a perfectly compact overture to set the scene. Bonham and Jones hold down a powerful and inventive rhythm section, and when the time comes, Jimmy flexes the Telecaster (played through a Leslie speaker to create that soaring effect) in a late Yardbirds-era fashion. From the onset

though, it's the Plant vocal that strikes home instantly. He executes all manner of vocal somersaults with the lyric but never loses control. Aided by a catchy chorus, 'Good Times Bad Times' is one of their most commercial offerings, and was at one time considered for release as their début single.

Live performances: *Never an integral part of their set, 'Good Times Bad Times' was featured on their début tour of Scandinavia, and resurfaced on their late 1969 set as an opening instrumental riff link for 'Communication Breakdown'. On the sixth US tour in the late summer of 1970, it returned as a vocal version inserted in the 'Communication Breakdown' medley and it made a brief return to the set during the 'Whole Lotta Love' medley played at their début show in Japan at the Budokan on September 23, 1971, and in Osaka on September 29, 1971.*

BABE I'M GONNA LEAVE YOU
TRADITIONAL – ARRANGED BY PAGE
(REMASTERS CREDITS – ANNE BREDON/PAGE)
STUDIO: OLYMPIC

This was a number Page played to Plant from a Joan Baez album during their initial meeting at Jimmy's riverside home at Pangbourne in August 1968. It was then that he first suggested covering the song with his new-found singing partner. When it came to recording, Jimmy rearranged this traditional folk tune to fit both acoustic and electric moulds. Thus, it emerges as an early example of their musical diversity, combining the energy of a forceful Plant vocal, and a strident crash-cymbal driven chorus, with some superbly picked Spanish guitar. It was one of the few tracks on the first album to use overdubs, and is also an early flowering of Robert's much repeated 'Baby, baby, baby' vocal mannerism.

Outtake versions reveal that Plant originally approached the song with a very forceful vocal. Page, however, opted for light and shade dynamics and this required Plant to apply his softer approach on the released version as well as the more strident tones.

Though credited as a traditional arrangement, the song was actually written by an American songwriter called Anne Bredon whose own performance had been adopted by Joan Baez for her interpretation. In the early Eighties Bredon challenged Atlantic with her claim and this was accepted. There was a change of credit on the 'Remasters' albums and a substantial back-payment in royalties for her.

Live performances: *Used on the initial 1968/69 tours and then discarded after the second US tour. A particularly vibrant version exists from their Danish TV special filmed in March 1969.*

YOU SHOOK ME
WILLIE DIXON
STUDIO: OLYMPIC

It's often forgotten just how heavily the early Led Zeppelin relied on the blues for inspiration. Their launch coincided with the British blues boom of 1968, and as can be seen from this showcase, they felt very at home in the company of standards like 'You Shook Me'. Robert in particular revelled in the song, extending the style he had perfected in The

Band Of Joy to great effect. Instrumentally, the track certainly packs some punch. From Jones' swirling organ, through Plant's harmonica wailing to the point where Jimmy's solo cascades around Bonzo's stereo panned tom tom attack, this is prime vintage Zeppelin. And the final incessant by-play between Page and Plant that leads out of the track is a masterful production technique, and one that would be further emphasised on stage.

'You Shook Me' also appeared on The Jeff Beck Group's album 'Truth'. Released a few months before the début Led Zeppelin album, Beck has gone on record as stating that Jimmy copied their arrangement for his own devices and was well upset when the Zeppelin album stormed the charts.

Live performances: *Featured on all the early 1968/69 tours, and was then deleted for the late 1969 US tour. Revived for the US, Japan, UK and Australian dates in 1971/72, when it was part of the 'Whole Lotta Love' medley. A brief reprise of the song was tagged on to the end of 'In My Time Of Dying' at Earls Court, and on the 1977 US tour.*

DAZED AND CONFUSED
PAGE
STUDIO: OLYMPIC

Originates from the mid-Sixties, when it was known as an acoustic folk tune sung by Jake Holmes. In The Yardbirds, Jimmy arranged it as 'I'm Confused' and it was played live on stage and on radio sessions. For the début album, Page added new lyrics, and spiced up the arrangement to extend the guitar played with violin bow episode. It still retains an air of menace and drama, and crystallises the electricity developing between the four at that time. It also beautifully illustrates Jones' walking bass style that lights up the track from start to finish.

Live performances: *A cornerstone of every Led Zeppelin live show until 1975. It became a vehicle for intensive improvisation, often encompassing snippets of other songs. These included Plant vocal ad libs of 'Woodstock', 'Spanish Eyes', The Eagles' 'Take It Easy' and Scott Mackenzie's 'San Francisco', plus Page riffing out on 'The Crunge', 'Walter's Walk' and 'West Side Story'. It also often stretched to 30 minutes in length. On the 1975 US tour,* the number had to be dropped for the first two weeks, when Jimmy injured his finger just before the tour. It made its reappearance during a stunning show at Madison Square Garden in New York on February 3. For the 1977 tour dates and Copenhagen/Knebworth in 1979, the violin bow section was extracted from 'Dazed And Confused' to form the visual centrepiece of the set. This section was also used with The Firm and on Page's solo 'Outrider' tour.

YOUR TIME IS GONNA COME
PAGE, JONES
STUDIO: OLYMPIC

Opening with a grand church organ display from Jones, this track builds into a hypnotic fade-out chorus, sung by all four members. Plant's phrasing throughout is superb – 'You been bad to me woman, but it's comin' back home to you'– and Jimmy overlays some tasteful pedal steel guitar. It all evaporates beautifully into the next cut .

Live performances: *Played on the first tour but then dropped. Made a one-off appearance in a medley of 'Whole Lotta Love' at the Budokan in Tokyo on September 24, 1971.*

BLACK MOUNTAIN SIDE
PAGE
STUDIO: OLYMPIC

The melody on this Page virtuoso acoustic guitar instrumental owes more than a passing nod to an old folk song recorded by both Bert Jansch and John Renbourn, known as 'Black Waterside'. Accompanied by the tabla playing of Viram Jasnai, Jimmy wades through a pleasing interlude that acts as light relief before the energy level clocks back up. Incidentally, Jimmy plays a borrowed Gibson J200 acoustic.

Page's Indian influence, also heard on 'White Summer', is on display here. During interviews for the 'Remasters' albums, Page referred to CIA tuning (Celtic, Indian and Arabic) – DADGAD – which would later be employed for 'Kashmir'.

Live Performances: *Incorporated into the Page/Yardbirds solo number 'White Summer' on all gigs up to the fifth US jaunt in 1970. Restored to the set for the 1977 US tour, Copenhagen and Knebworth in 1979 and the 'Over Europe' tour in 1980. It later emerged in the Firm era composition 'Midnight Moonlight' and part of this number was revived by Page on his 'Outrider' tour of 1988.*

COMMUNICATION BREAKDOWN
PAGE, JONES, BONHAM
STUDIO: OLYMPIC

An early Led Zeppelin anthem, this track grew out of their Scandinavian set when it dove-tailed into the similar tempoed show opener 'Train Kept A-Rollin''. A brilliant example of Page's ability to create a whole song around a repeated guitar riff, 'Communication Breakdown' is a storming rocker that peaks just around the point Plant screams 'Suck it!' and Page cuts a screeching guitar path across the speakers. It has survived the test of time to become one of the true all time greats of the Zeppelin catalogue.

Live performances: *Developing during their first tour in September 1968, it went on to be a lasting part of their show. It was used on all dates in 1969, and in 1970 it was elevated to encore status. On the sixth US tour it was used as an encore medley. It subsequently appeared as an encore on each successive tour, including the last night at Earls Court, and the second Knebworth date. It was again an encore special for Europe 1980, and was part of Plant's 1988 and 1990 solo set. This was also the number they played on their only live UK TV appearance in March 1969.*

I CAN'T QUIT YOU BABY
WILLIE DIXON
STUDIO: OLYMPIC

Another slow Willie Dixon blues, this is notable for its ambient production quality that brings to the fore John Bonham's wonderfully laid-back drumming, and Jimmy's deceptively mellow guitar sparring. There's a great 'just having a blow' atmosphere about this track that makes for a very relaxed outing.

Live performances: *Included in their set from 1968 up to the fifth US tour in 1970. Revived as part of the 'Whole Lotta Love' medley on the Japan, UK and Europe tours 1972/3. This track was also rehearsed for the Atlantic 40th Anniversary reunion in May 1988, but was not included on the night. Page and Plant performed a short version of this song at the Hammersmith show a month earlier.*

HOW MANY MORE TIMES
PAGE, JONES, BONHAM
STUDIO: OLYMPIC

The closing number of their early stage act and appropriately enough the parting shot of their début album, 'How Many More Times' is a lengthy, high energy exit. Along the way all sorts of playful things occur. From the suitably dramatic intro, complete with stinging Page wah-wah, the track develops into a medley of its own. Apparently the appearance of 'Rosie' and 'The Hunter' came spontaneously on the night of the session itself. Plant is quite fantastic here. He comes on as a supremely confident carnal gourmet boasting of much excess, but with a smile never too far from his lips.

Note also Page's bowing technique. Alongside 'Dazed And Confused', this track has its origins in the old Yardbirds repertoire.

Live performances: *'How Many More Times' held down the closing slot in the Zeppelin set up to and including their 1970 Bath Festival appearance. It reappeared briefly on the Japan 1971 dates, and at a date at Southampton University in January 1973. It came back into the set for the 1975 US tour, when it replaced 'Dazed And Confused' for the first two weeks due to Jimmy's injured finger.*

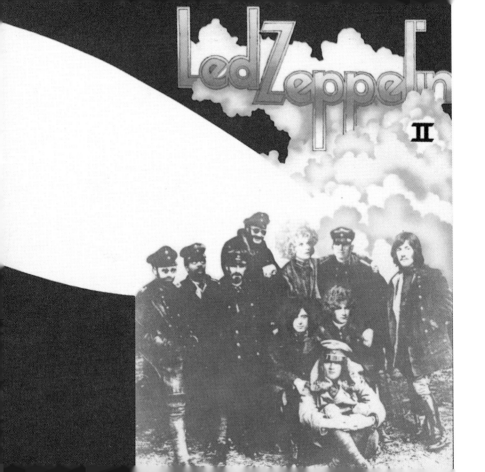

LED ZEPPELIN ii

ATLANTIC RECORDS
ORIGINAL ISSUE 588 198, RE-ISSUE K40087

Little time was lost between the recording of their début and the sessions that would result in the follow-up. 'Led Zeppelin II' was the group's first introduction to engineer Eddie Kramer whose work with Jimi Hendrix had already impressed Page, but studio time had to be grabbed between months of intense touring, principally in the US.

Consequently all manner of primitive studios were tried. Jimmy can recall one eight track set-up in Vancouver that didn't even boast proper headphone facilities. That the album turned out to be such a triumph, in particular for a production quality that still sounds fresh today, was in no small way due to the successful alliance of Page and Kramer in the control room.

One of the more successful studios Zeppelin entered for the second album was Mystic in Hollywood. Page had previously recorded there for the 'Lord Sutch And Heavy Friends' album, and he returned with his new group to lay down 'The Lemon Song' completely live in Mystic's 16x16 foot room. "It had wooden walls and lots of ambience,"

Page recalls. "It was a small room. Richie Valens and Bobby Fuller had once recorded there, and when you listen to those Fifties records you can tell it's a small room, but the energy of it comes through."

A further round of recording at Olympic and Morgan studios in London, with Kramer and assistants Andy Johns and George Chkiantz, completed the basic tracks which were then mixed over one weekend by Page and Kramer in New York. "The famous 'Whole Lotta Love' mix, where everything is going bananas, is a combination of Jimmy and myself just flying around on a small console twiddling every knob known to man," says Kramer.

In between the harder-edged material, however, there were some examples of the ever widening scope of the group's intentions. This album also marked the emergence of Robert Plant as a serious songwriter. His name had been notably absent from the début album credits due to previous contractual commitments that resulted from his association with CBS Records. Now, his influence on tracks such as 'What Is And What Should Never Be' and 'Ramble On' were definite pointers to the musical future of Led Zeppelin.

'Led Zeppelin II' was released on October 31, 1969. In America it had advance orders for half a million copies. It entered the *Billboard* chart at 15, and by the end of the year it had dislodged The Beatles' 'Abbey Road' to take the top spot, where it remained for seven weeks. By April 1970 it had registered three million American sales. It was a similar success story at home. On November 8, 1969, it began a 138-week residency on the LP chart, climbing to the top spot in February 1970.

The sleeve design was based on a David Juniper poster, and the advertising campaign was built around the slogan 'Led Zeppelin II Now Flying'. The cover illustration was based on an archive photo of the Jasta Division of the German air force with the four faces of the

members of the group airbrushed on from a much used 1969 Atlantic publicity photo.

'Led Zeppelin II' marks a very creative period for the group, and it remains a nostalgic reflection of the sheer exuberance inspired by the intensive tour schedule aimed (successfully) at conquering America.

WHOLE LOTTA LOVE
PAGE, BONHAM, PLANT, JONES
STUDIOS: OLYMPIC; SUNSET SOUND, LOS ANGELES; A AND R, NEW YORK

The catalyst. A masterful Page/Kramer production. From Plant's off-mike cough through to the 'Keepa coolin' baby' squeals, this is five minutes and 33 seconds of aural and sexual delight. The song originally took shape around Page's killer three-note riff with its octave E conclusion, and a descending chord structure which employed backwards echo effects first used by Jimmy on a Mickie Most session. Devoid of any lyrics of their own, Plant took some from Willie Dixon's 'You Need Love'. In failing to credit Dixon, the group were subsequently sued and they settled out of court.

But the most impressive part of 'Whole

Lotta Love' had nothing whatsoever to do with Willie Dixon. This was the apocalyptic central section in which Page mixed all manner of crazy sound effects – full tilt whoops, screams, sirens and demolition noises interspersed with what sounded remarkably like Robert squealing in orgasmic bliss from the depths of a coal mine – into a truly mindblowing sequence which careered wildly from speaker to speaker and suggested total mayhem.

This section was missing – inevitably – when 'Whole Lotta Love' was edited down to become a Top Five hit single in America. It also reached number one in Belgium and Germany. In the UK, Atlantic had expected to issue the edited version themselves, and pressed initial copies for release on December 5, 1969. However, Peter Grant halted the release, stating that to issue singles off albums was not Led Zeppelin's policy. An official statement added that they had written a special number which they intended to be their first British single. This never materialised, and despite much record company pressure, they declined to issue official singles in the UK throughout their career.

In many respects 'Whole Lotta Love' would become a millstone around Led Zeppelin's collective neck. An instrumental version of the song by CCS (aka Collective Consciousness Society), a large studio group put together by Alexis Korner and Danish bluesman Peter Thorup, became the signature tune for the UK weekly TV chart show *Top Of The Pops*, thus ensuring that it would seep into the consciousness of every pop fan in the land, whether or not they were fans of Led Zeppelin.

It also came to be regarded – quite rightly – as the definitive expression of heavy metal, a term of reference yet to come into common usage when 'Led Zeppelin II' was released, and as a result Led Zeppelin would eventually become known as the definitive heavy metal band. It was a pejorative description they would come to abhor, which they would never be able to shake off, and which they certainly didn't deserve. They were not to know how many thousands of future bands would rip off the concept of 'Whole Lotta Love' – the directness of a repeated riff awash in echo – in the years to come or how many bands would take their style and look, simplify it for easy access, mass consumption and sheer escapism, and refer to it and themselves as heavy metal. Musical eclecticism was Led Zeppelin's real hallmark, and that eclecticism incorporated much more than the simple yet explosive noise that was 'Whole Lotta Love'.

Live performances: *'Whole Lotta Love' made its live début on the second US tour in April 1969. In June 1969 they previewed it on a BBC session. It was then part of each subsequent set list. For the early 1970 dates it was an encore number. From the sixth US tour in 1970 up to the 1973 US tour, it was the closing finale of every Zeppelin performance, extending in length to include a rock'n'roll medley. On their 1975 dates it was an encore medley with 'Black Dog' and in 1977 it was used as a medley encore with 'Rock And Roll' and, on one occasion at the LA Forum, with 'Communication Breakdown'. It was given a new arrangement for the 1979 Copenhagen/Knebworth encores (the same version was revived for the Atlantic 40th Anniversary reunion in May 1988), and returned to the 'Let That Boy Boogie' medley workout for the 1980 Europe dates. It holds the distinction of*

being the last track Led Zeppelin performed live, when it received a 17-minute work-out at the final gig in Berlin on July 7, 1980. It was also played at the Live Aid get- together on July 13, 1985.

WHAT IS AND WHAT SHOULD NEVER BE
PAGE, PLANT
STUDIOS: OLYMPIC; GROOVE, NEW YORK; A AND R

The genesis of Robert Plant's career as a songwriter, this dreamy affair is a marked departure from the dizzy atmosphere of 'Whole Lotta Love'. It's also another superb Page production with its flanging vocal effects and powerful stereo separation on the fade out. Jimmy had now switched to the Gibson Les Paul for recording, and the sustained solo here is really quite beautiful.

Live performances: *Previewed in June 1969 on a BBC radio session, premièred at the London Lyceum on October 12 and then inserted on the late 1969 US tour and played at every gig through 1970/71 up to the US tour in June 1972. Discarded thereafter.*

THE LEMON SONG
CHESTER BURNETT
STUDIOS: MYSTIC, LOS ANGELES; A AND R

This track was originally credited to Page, Plant, Jones and Bonham but claims from publishers Jewel Music that the song was heavily based on Chester (Howlin' Wolf) Burnett's 'Killing Floor' led to another settlement and a change of sleeve credit. In fact, some later copies of the album do list the track as 'Killing Floor'. This arrangement also takes from Albert King's 'Cross-Cut Saw', a staple of the gigs Plant would perform with The Honeydrippers in 1981. Recorded virtually live in New York's Mystic studios, the track combined 'Killing Floor', which they had been performing at their early gigs, with the Robert Johnson inspired 'squeeze my lemon' sequence with its intense erotic overtones.

Live performances: *'Killing Floor' was used on the début American tour, and was to evolve into 'The Lemon Song' for the second and third tours. Dropped in late 1969, though the 'squeeze my lemon' sequence was often inserted into the 'Whole Lotta Love' medley and ad-libbed elsewhere.*

THANK YOU
PAGE, PLANT
STUDIOS: MORGAN, LONDON; A AND R

This emotional love song to his wife brings out the best in Robert Plant, as he commits to tape one of his finest vocal performances. Elsewhere in the arrangement John Paul Jones excels on Hammond organ, and Jimmy complements it all with some delicate Rickenbacker 12-string picking.

Live performances: *Made its début in the set on the January 1970 UK tour. Stayed in the show throughout 1970/71 acting as a spotlight for Jonesy's keyboard solo. Used as a marathon encore on the 1972/3 tours and then deleted from the act. At the Freddie Mercury Tribute Concert at Wembley Stadium in April 1992, Plant sang a few lines from the song as a bridge intro to his version of Queen's 'Crazy Little Thing Called Love'.*

HEARTBREAKER
PAGE, PLANT, JONES, BONHAM
STUDIO: A&R

'Heartbreaker' is another integral part of the recorded Zeppelin canon and a perfect platform for Page to display his guitar virtuosity. On this studio cut, he offers up a breathtaking exercise in string-bending guitar technique, while on the road he extended the track to include snippets of Bach's Lute Suite No.1 and Simon and Garfunkel's '59th Street Bridge Song'.

Live performances: *A long-standing live fave, it joined the set at the Lyceum in October 1969. From the Bath Festival onwards and throughout the rest of their dates in 1970/71, it provided a dual thrust set opener with 'Immigrant Song'. For the US, Japan, UK and Europe tours of 1972/73, it became part of the encore. It was back in the main set as a medley with 'Whole Lotta Love' for the 1973 US dates (see* The Song Remains The Same *movie), and then an encore again on the 1975 US tour, the last night at Earls Court, selected dates during the 1977 US tour, Knebworth 1, and the Europe 1980 tour. It was also per-*

formed at the Atlantic 40th Anniversary reunion in 1988.

Additional colouring that Page brought to this track included a few chords from 'Greensleeves' and a regular instrumental passage based on Bach's 'Bourée' in C minor'. When employed as an encore during the 1975 US tour, versions of 'That's Alright' and 'I'm A Man' were inserted into the song at Madison Square Garden (Feb 12) and Long Beach (March 12) respectively.

LIVIN' LOVIN' MAID (SHE'S JUST A WOMAN)
PAGE, PLANT
STUDIOS: MORGAN, LONDON;
A AND R, NEW YORK

Jimmy returned to the Telecaster to knock out what the band always considered to be something of a production line filler. However, this tight, hook-laden ditty, found much favour on the radio, and when 'Whole Lotta Love' finished its chart run in America, 'Livin' Lovin' Maid' was flipped over to become an A-side in its own right. It then climbed to Number 65 on the *Billboard* chart. The song is rumoured to

be about one of their early, persistent West Coast groupies.

Live performances: *Such was their distaste for this track, it never received a full public airing. On a date in Hamburg in March 1970 Plant slipped the first line of the song into 'Heartbreaker' and he sang the opening line in jest at Earls Court on May 24, 1975. Explaining the intention of this show he said, "We don't just mean we're gonna groove around on anything that could be groovy like 'With the purple umbrella and the 50 cent hat' no... none of that!" In a surprise move Plant brought the song into his 'Manic Nirvana' US solo tour set in 1990, turning it into a rousing encore with a mock Beach Boys arrangement.*

RAMBLE ON
PAGE, PLANT
STUDIOS: JUGGY SOUND; A AND R

Enter the ethereal Page and Plant. 'Ramble On', with its Tolkien-inspired lyrical content was for Plant in particular the highlight of 'Led Zeppelin II'. It remains a splendid illustration of the light and shade dynamism that would char-

acterise so much of their future work. It slips effortlessly from quiet mournful passages into an uplifting chorus, and Page's overdubbed interweaving Gibson run is an early attempt at the guitar army assault.

Live performances: *Surprisingly, 'Ramble On' was never performed live in a full version. On the Spring 1970 US tour Plant did throw in lines from the song during 'Communication Breakdown' (see 'Mudslide' bootleg) and 'Whole Lotta Love'.*

MOBY DICK
BONHAM, JONES, PAGE
STUDIOS: MIRROR SOUND, L.A.; MAY FAIR, NEW YORK; A AND R

John Bonham's percussive showcase took shape on the second US tour when it was known as 'Pat's Delight' (a reference to his wife). Built between a killer Page riff, which was used as the theme to BBC 2's *Disco 2* rock show, Bonzo does his thing with sticks and bare hands.

Outtakes from the 'Zeppelin II' sessions reveal the 'Moby Dick' drums solo to have been edited down from a much longer version. The riff part of the track can be traced back to the BBC unused session track 'The Girl I Love' which was laid down in the summer of 1969.

Live performances: *Came in on the 1969 November US tour and stayed in the set on every tour up to 1977 although it was not played at every single show. It developed into an excessive 20-minute showcase which provided the others with a break in the show. By 1975 Bonzo was incorporating a 'Whole Lotta Love' riff segment played on electronically treated kettle drums. On the 1977 US tour, the track was aptly renamed 'Over The Top', and employed the riff of 'Out On The Tiles' instead of the 'Moby Dick' theme.*

Live performances: *Used on stage from the November 1969 US tour and retained for their 1970 itinerary. Live, it developed into a lengthy piece with a great Page/ Bonham guitar-drum battle. Revived briefly for the 1972 US tour as an encore and re-employed on the 1973 US tour as an opening sequence riff link to merge 'Celebration Days' with 'Black Dog', 'Bring It On Home' was also played at the reunion staged at Jason Bonham's wedding reception in May 1990.*

BRING IT ON HOME
PAGE, PLANT
STUDIOS: MYSTIC, LOS ANGELES; ATLANTIC, NEW YORK; A AND R

Opening with a straight lift from Sonny Boy Williamson's 'Bring It On Home' it soon snaps into electric action, but it's a rather hackneyed blues rocker that always worked better live.

LED ZEPPELIN iii

ATLANTIC RECORDS

ORIGINAL ISSUE 2401002, RE-ISSUE K50002

After the often absurd studio conditions enduring for the second album, the group made a conscious effort to alter the pace of future recording. Fortunately their strategy for self-sufficiency had paid off in spades, and it was most unlikely that there would ever be a repeat of the pressures that caused them to record as hurriedly as they had in 1969. Fate, as we shall see, would change all that down the line but in the meantime their third album could be approached at a considerably more leisurely pace.

Page and Plant set the ball rolling with their much documented trip to Bron-Y-Aur, a remote cottage in Snowdonia where they could play and compose into the night, working by candlelight and the soft glow of a wood fire. Such surroundings – and the lack of electric power – not unnaturally signalled a slight change of direction with an emphasis on acoustic arrangements.

After preparing the material that would emerge on 'Led Zeppelin III', they rehearsed the songs at a run-down mansion in Hampshire. This proved to be a significant move. With its relaxed atmosphere and rural surroundings, Headley Grange provided a favoured alternative to the discipline of a conventional studio.

The third album was recorded in a series of May/June sessions at Headley Grange and Olympic with Andy Johns engineering. Some additional work was put in at the newly opened Island Studios in London's Notting Hill in July. It was all wrapped up with a mixdown at Ardent Studios in Memphis during Zeppelin's sixth American tour in August 1970.

The whole album proved to be a watershed release, not only in content and construction, but also in composition. After Page's domination of the first two albums, the third was a more democratic affair, and given increased rehearsal time, all four group members were able to offer up their own compositions and ideas. It was a pattern that would continue in future sessions.

'Led Zeppelin III' was the most eagerly awaited album of 1970. After what was to become a traditional Led Zeppelin delay (this time two months), it finally surfaced in October of that year. Advance orders in America were close to the million mark, and it spent four weeks at the top of the *Billboard* chart. It entered the British chart at number one and remained there for three weeks. It returned to the top for a further week on December 12.

The elaborate gatefold sleeve, which held up release, was designed by Richard Drew, a lecturer in fine arts at Leeds Polytechnic. Its rotating inner wheel, an idea of Page's, was based on crop rotation charts but the end result was not quite how Jimmy had originally conceived it. Its release was trailered by a full page ad taken out in the *Melody Maker* at the end of September. In a reference to their run-away success in that year's *Melody Maker* readers' poll, the ad simply said, 'Thank you for making us the world's number one band.'

The diverse content of the album, with its accent on more acoustically based arrange-ments, confused both critics and the public alike. Hindsight was to prove that this change in direction was a natural progression for the group. At no point would they restrict them-selves to one musical genre.

'Led Zeppelin III' is another triumph for Jimmy Page as a producer. He brings out the best qualities of each song here, from the dra-matic intro of 'Since I've Been Loving You' through to the delicacy of 'That's The Way'. It all adds up to one of their most absorbing and intimate listening experiences.

IMMIGRANT SONG
PAGE, PLANT

STUDIOS: HEADLEY GRANGE, HAMPSHIRE;
ISLAND AND OLYMPIC, LONDON; ARDENT, MEMPHIS

Nothing less than a classic. Built around an incessant Page/Jones/Bonham battering riff, this Plant tale of Viking lust is a compulsive attack on the senses as well as a call to arms. In addition to containing some of Plant's most memorable lines, it also boasts a wailing war-cry destined to delight rabid audiences across the world.

The basis of this track was already recorded before their trip to play in Iceland on June 22, 1970. It was this vacation that inspired Robert to construct a new set of lyrics full of Icelandic imagery. As he put it in a 1970 radio interview: "We went to Iceland, and it made you think of Vikings and big ships... and John Bonham's stomach... and bang, there it was – Immigrant Song!"

The count in at the start, by the way, is coupled with echo tape feedback – hence the hiss. In America 'Immigrant Song' was lifted as a single and after a 13-week chart run peaked at 16.

Live performances: *'Immigrant Song' was premièred to UK audiences at the opening of Led Zeppelin's 1970 Bath Festival appearance. This version features varying verses to the later studio issue. The live arrangement included an extended guitar solo. It was the set opener of every show played from Bath 1970 up to the 1972 US tour. For the Japan, UK and Europe 1972/73 dates it emerged as part of the encore. It was then deleted from the set. One odd live improvisation occurred on August 22, 1971, at the LA Forum when 'Immigrant Song' opened the set and Page prefaced the intro with a few bars of The Ventures' 'Walk Don't Run'. Robert Plant was to revive the song in an amended arrangement on his solo tours of 1988/1990.*

FRIENDS
PAGE, PLANT
STUDIOS: ISLAND; HEADLEY GRANGE; ARDENT

A few seconds of studio chat precedes this hypnotic swirling mass of sound. It's surprising that John Paul Jones has no composing credit here, as he is wholly responsible for the track's compelling string arrangement. There's a Moog synthesiser added on the outro which provides a link to the next track. With its repeated acoustic guitar motifs and bongo percussion, this bizarre outing was unlike anything else they attempted.

Page used an Altair Tube Limiter to enhance the acoustic quality of his Harmony guitar, a device recommended by Dick Rosemenie, an acoustic guitarist who recorded an album entitled 'Six String, Twelve String and Vanguard'. The same device was used on 'All My Love' on the 'In Through The Out Door' album.

'Friends' employs another odd tuning. Jimmy: "Top E is E, B is a C, G is a G, D is a C, A remains the same, and the low E goes down to C. We also did that on 'Bron-Y-Aur' and 'Poor Tom'."

Live performances: *The only documented live performance of 'Friends' is a version played in Osaka on the 1971 Japanese tour. This was also, along with 'Four Sticks', one of the experimental songs Jimmy and Robert recorded with the Bombay Orchestra in March 1972.*

CELEBRATION DAY
PAGE, PLANT, JONES
STUDIOS: HEADLEY GRANGE; ISLAND; ARDENT

A track that nearly didn't appear at all. Due to a studio oversight, the intro of this track was crinkled on the master tape, making it impossible to thread, but by segueing the swirling link from 'Friends' into the guitar riff and Plant's opening lyrics, the song was salvaged. A good thing too, as it's an excellent vehicle for a succession of Page's guitar effects, and Plant's happy tour of New York.

Live performances: *Came in to the set as part of a medley with 'Communication Breakdown' at the KB Hallen date in Copenhagen in the spring of 1971, then used on the late summer tour of America in 1971, and stayed for the Japanese, UK and Australian tours of late 1971 early 1972. Revived for the 1973 US dates and then again for the Copenhagen and Knebworth gigs in 1979.*

SINCE I'VE BEEN LOVING YOU
PAGE, PLANT
STUDIOS: ISLAND; ARDENT

One of the first songs prepared for 'Zeppelin III', it was previewed as early as the January tour of the UK in 1970. A self-styled and somewhat mannered slow blues, with some lovely organ from J.P., it featured one of Jimmy's most expressive solos prefaced by a dramatic shout of 'Watch out!' from Plant.

Live performances: *Entered the set in early 1970 and retained throughout their 1970/71 dates. From the Japan tour in 1972 up to the 1973 American dates, it formed the second half of a medley with 'Misty Mountain Hop'. It came back into the set in its own right for the latter part of the 1975 US tour, and reappeared for the 1977 US tour, Copenhagen/Knebworth 1979, and Europe 1980. On Plant's solo tours part of the track was aired in 'Slow Dancer'. Also performed in a version at Hammersmith in 1988 with Page guesting.*

OUT ON THE TILES
PAGE, PLANT, BONHAM
STUDIOS: ISLAND; OLYMPIC; ARDENT, MEMPHIS

After Page's domination of the first two albums, the more leisurely paced recording of 'Zeppelin III' allowed for a more democratic pool of ideas. This track came out of a Bonham-inspired riff and is a much underrated part of their output. With an infectious chorus and enthusiastic Plant vocal, it bubbles along with an unnerving energy. The title relates to a previously written set of lyrics that were revamped for this version. The spacey sound mix evident here is another example of distance miking in the studio by Page.

Live performances: *This track was only ever used on the sixth US tour of September 1970. However, the opening riff was later applied to the live arrangement of 'Black Dog'. Then on the 1977 US tour the riff structure of 'Out On The Tiles' replaced 'Moby Dick' as the lead intro to Bonham's drum solo which was retitled by Plant as 'Over The Top'.*

GALLOWS POLE
TRADITIONAL: ARRANGED BY PAGE & PLANT
STUDIOS: HEADLEY GRANGE; ISLAND; ARDENT

This traditional folk tune can be traced back to Leadbelly. His version titled 'Gallis Pole' can be found on 'The Leadbelly Story' (DVRECD 39). Another version is on an album by Odetta, 'The Leadbelly Essential Odetta' (Vanguard VCD 43/44). Other blues variations of the tune of the song have been recorded as 'Gallows Line' and 'Maid Freed From the Gallows'. Jimmy adapted it from a version by Fred Gerlach.

Instrumentally, it has Page on banjo, six and 12 acoustic guitar and electric guitar. John Paul Jones is on mandolin and bass. While Plant unfolds a tale of medieval woe, the tension builds beautifully as Bonzo wades in, and Page adds an understated but frenzied Gibson run. One of their most adventurous outings and quite brilliant in its execution – lyrically and musically.

Live performances: *Played on some of the March/May UK and European tour dates in 1971. Robert did sometimes throw in some lines of this during 'Trampled Underfoot',* remarking on its performance on the last night of the 1975 US tour in LA as being 'Trampled Under Gallows'.

TANGERINE
PAGE
STUDIOS: HEADLEY GRANGE; OLYMPIC; ARDENT

Jimmy provides an eight-second count-in to a mellow solo composition left over from his Yardbirds era. Robert duets with himself on a double-tracked vocal, and Pagey layers on some tasteful pedal steel guitar.

Live performances: *Joined the acoustic set on the Japanese dates in September 1971. Remained in the set on all tours up to the US dates in the summer of 1972. Revived as a four-part harmony rendition for the Earls Court season in 1975, for which Jimmy pulled out the Gibson double-neck.*

THAT'S THE WAY
PAGE, PLANT
STUDIOS: ISLAND; ARDENT

One of their very best performances and definitely Robert's best ever lyric, 'That's The Way' carried the working title of 'The Boy Next Door'. It was written at the cottage in Bron-Y-Aur, and centres around the dissolution of a pair of star crossed lovers. The lyrics were influenced in part by the unrest Robert witnessed on their Spring 1970 US travels. The tale unfolds against a rush of acoustic guitars, and a moving horn-like electric solo from Jimmy.

Live performances: *Premièred at Bath, and a standard feature of the acoustic set during 1970/71 and up to the American tour in 1972. Recalled for the Earls Court season in 1975.*

BRON-Y-AUR STOMP
PAGE, PLANT, JONES
STUDIOS: HEADLEY GRANGE; ISLAND; ARDENT

Some light relief. A playful folksy singalong, written at the cottage about Plant's dog Strider. Page gets in some fine picking, Bonzo adds spoons and castanets, and Jones plays an acoustic bass. The tune itself was tried in an electric rockier arrangement at the commencement of the third album sessions late in 1969, when it was known as 'Jennings Farm Blues'.

Live performances: *Used in the acoustic set from the UK dates in Spring 1971 through to the American tour in 1972. A revamped arrangement with Jonesy on stand-up bass was used for the Japan/UK/Europe 1972/73 dates. Recalled in this format for Earls Court in 1975, and then as a medley with 'Black Country Woman' on the 1977 US tour.*

HATS OFF TO (ROY) HARPER
TRADITIONAL; ARRANGED BY CHARLES OBSCURE
STUDIOS: ISLAND; OLYMPIC; ARDENT

Nothing more than a Page/Plant jam, loosely based on Bukka White's old blues tune 'Shake 'Em On Down'. Page does get in some fairly authentic bottleneck guitar but it's hardly essential listening. The title is a bold acknowledgement of their admiration for the eccentric Mr H. A six-minute, similar styled blues medley was also recorded during this session which also featured 'That's All Right Mama' and Country Joe's 'Feel Like I'm Fixin' To Die Rag'.

Live performances: *None.*

ATLANTIC RECORDS
ORIGINAL ISSUE 2401 OZ 2, RE-ISSUE K50008

When Led Zeppelin returned to Headley Grange in early 1971, they took along The Rolling Stones' mobile studio to record the whole process. "We needed the sort of facilities where we could have a cup of tea and wander around the garden and then go in and do what we had to do," said Page. By moving into Headley Grange for the whole period of recording, many of the tracks were made up almost on the spot and committed to tape almost there and then.

"A recording studio is an immediate imposition as compared to sitting around a fire strumming," said Robert Plant at the time. "With Headley Grange we can put something down and hear the results immediately."

Initial sessions for the fourth album began at the new Island studios in December 1970, but the real work was done in the country. Once inside the great hall of Headley Grange, ideas flowed freely. It was here that Page stumbled on that monster snare and bass drum sound by spaciously miking Bonzo's newly acquired kit.

With the basic tracks recorded, many of them live, they added overdubs at Island and on the recommendation of engineer Andy Johns took the completed master tapes to Los Angeles Sunset Sound Studios for mixing. This mix proved to be a great disappointment, causing a delay in the release of the album. They had hoped to have it out in time for their late summer tour of the US, but further mixing back in London put the release back to November.

After the mixed reception that greeted 'Led Zeppelin III', the group deliberately played down the release of their fourth album. There had been talk of releasing a double set at one time, and at one stage Jimmy came up with the idea of issuing the fourth album as four EPs.

When it came to a title, instead of the expected 'Led Zeppelin IV', they decided to set a precedent by selecting four symbols, each representing a member of the band, to form the title. Each member chose his own symbol. John Bonham's came from a book of runes and took the form of three linked circles. Said to represent the man-wife-child trilogy, Plant was heard to remark that it resembled the emblem of Ballantine beer! John Paul Jones' came from the same book and is meant to represent confidence and compe-

tence. Plant's feather in a circle design was his own, based on the sign of the ancient Mu civilisation. Jimmy Page's mysterious symbol, which has often been mistaken for a word that could be pronounced 'Zoso', was also his own work. The group could hardly have known at the time what lasting imagery these symbols would have on their following.

To further throw the media (and the music industry, their fans and everyone else!), the gatefold sleeve design was entirely wordless except for a barely decipherable Oxfam poster hanging amidst the urban decay depicted on the front. This cover print was actually bought from a junk shop in Reading by Plant. A tarot card illustration of the Hermit formed the inner gatefold illustration and the lyrics to 'Stairway To Heaven' were printed on the inner sleeve. Atlantic Records' reaction to this total lack of information on the sleeve was predictably negative.

As a result of all this mystery, no-one has ever been quite sure what to actually call the album, and it has been variously referred to over the years as 'Led Zeppelin IV', 'Untitled', 'Four Symbols', 'Zoso' and 'The Runes'. And since no-one from the Zeppelin camp has ever actually confirmed a title, the mystery is unlikely ever to be solved. Which is exactly what the increasingly mysterious Led Zeppelin wanted!

In the run up to the album's release, a series of teaser adverts depicting each symbol was placed in the music press. It did not take their fans too long to associate these mystical images with the album, and, title or no title, the fourth Zeppelin album was an instant massive seller. It entered the UK chart at number one and stayed on the chart for 62 weeks. In America it remained on the chart longer than any other Zeppelin album, though it failed to knock Carole King's mega-selling 'Tapestry' off the top. Ultimately the fourth Zeppelin album would be the most durable seller in their catalogue and the most impressive critical and commercial success of their career.

In December 1990, this album, along with Def Leppard's 'Hysteria', was certified by *Billboard* magazine as being the biggest selling rock album in American chart history. By that year's end it had registered some 10 million sales in the US alone. Not bad for an album whose wordless sleeve artwork was declared commercial suicide when it was first handed to the record company.

: THE TEN ALBUM LEGACY

BLACK DOG
PAGE, PLANT, JONES
STUDIOS: HEADLEY GRANGE, HAMPSHIRE, WITH THE
ROLLING STONES' MOBILE; ISLAND, LONDON

If 'Zeppelin III' had thrown up doubts in some corners as to their ability to still flex the power displayed on the first two albums, here was the perfect antidote. The moment Page warms up the Gibsons, this is one of the most instantly recognisable Zepp tracks.

The impossible part of the riff was a Jones input, while the *a cappella* vocal arrangement, Page would admit years later, was influenced by Fleetwood Mac's 'Oh Well'. The solo is constructed out of four overdubbed Les Paul fills. 'Black Dog' takes its title from a mutt that hung around at the Grange. It is held in great esteem in particular by Plant, who would later add snippets of the song into his solo tracks 'Tall Cool One', and 'Your Ma Said She Cried In Her Sleep Last Night'.

Live performances: *Joined the set on the UK tour at Belfast's Ulster Hall on March 5, 1971. Retained for each subsequent tour up to the 1973 US tour. Used as an encore medley with 'Whole Lotta Love' on the 1975 US tour and*

Earls Court. Hardly used in 1977 (the July 23 Oakland show saw its appearance as a rare second encore). Recalled to the set for the 1979 Copenhagen/Knebworth dates and Europe 1980 (complete with rare spoken intro from Jimmy).

ROCK AND ROLL
PAGE, PLANT, JONES, BONHAM
STUDIOS: HEADLEY GRANGE, WITH THE ROLLING
STONES' MOBILE; ISLAND; OLYMPIC

Another instantly identifiable Zeppelin anthem. This track came out of a jam with The Stones' mentor Ian Stewart on piano. Bonzo played the intro of 'Good Golly Miss Molly'/'Keep A Knockin'', and Page added a riff. Fifteen minutes later the nucleus of 'Rock And Roll' was down on tape – displaying the full benefit of recording on location with the tapes ever running.

Live performances: *A lasting part of their history, 'Rock And Roll' came in as an encore on the spring 1971 dates when it was referred to by Plant as 'It's Been A Long Time'. It was inserted into the main set for the US, Japanese, UK and Australian tour schedule of*

1971/2. When they revamped the set in late 1972 for the Japan and UK dates it was elevated to the opening number, probably because its first line – 'It's been a long time since I rock and rolled' – was highly appropriate for a show opener. It retained this status on every show up to the Earls Court season in 1975. It became a medley encore with 'Whole Lotta Love' in America in 1977. For Knebworth and Europe it was an encore in its own right. Post-Zeppelin, it has enjoyed airings at Live Aid, at Hammersmith with Plant and Page in 1988, at Jason Bonham's wedding bash, and The Knebworth Silver Clef reunion. It has also been a staple of US band Heart's live set.

THE BATTLE OF EVERMORE
PAGE, PLANT
STUDIOS: HEADLEY GRANGE WITH THE ROLLING STONES' MOBILE; OLYMPIC, LONDON

The tune for this was written by Page late one night at the Grange while he experimented on Jones' mandolin. Robert came up with a set of lyrics inspired by a book he was reading on the Scottish wars. Sandy Denny was called in to sing the answer lines to Plant's play-ette.

Another impressive arrangement. A solo Plant guide vocal outtake remains in the vaults.

This song appeared in the 1992 grunge cult film *Singles*, performed by The Love Mongers who featured Annie and Nancy Wilson of Heart.

Live performances: *Only ever played live on the 1977 US tour, with John Paul Jones taking on the dual vocal task.*

STAIRWAY TO HEAVEN
PAGE, PLANT
STUDIOS: HEADLEY GRANGE WITH THE ROLLING STONES' MOBILE; ISLAND

The big one. 'Stairway' started out as a fairly complete chord progression that Page brought in when they commenced recording at Island studios in December 1970. At Headley Grange the song developed around the log fire with Robert composing a set of lyrics full of hippy mysticism that told the tale of a search for spiritual perfection. The song's arrangement with Jones contributing bass recorder on the intro and Bonzo entering as the track built to a crescendo, came together very quickly. This left Jimmy to add the solo, for which he

returned to the Telecaster, back at Island. For the live version he would invest in a custom-made Gibson SG double-neck guitar.

'Stairway To Heaven' was undoubtedly the stand out track on the fourth album, and was well received when they performed it on the UK and US dates prior to the album's release. When they went back to the States in the summer of 1972, Atlantic were naturally keen to issue the track as a single. Grant refused

and was to do the same again the next year. The upshot of that decision was that record buyers began to invest in the fourth album as if it were a single.

'Stairway To Heaven' went on to become the most requested song on American radio, and achieve truly classic status worldwide. Far from being a mere rock song, it has become something of a people's favourite, cover version fodder for symphony orchestras and night club singers alike. So well known has the dreamy opening riff become that guitarists trying out guitars in music shops must pay a fine of £5 if they play 'Stairway' in the shop! In 1993 an entire album of cover versions of 'Stairway To Heaven' by various Australian performers instigated by the Australian *Money Or The Gun* TV show was released, and a spoof rendering by the inimitable Rolf Harris found its way into the UK Top Ten amid much jocularity.

Alongside songs like 'A Whiter Shade Of Pale' and 'You've Lost That Loving Feeling', 'Stairway' has a pastoral opening cadence that is classical in feel and which has ensured its immortality. This air of respectability may be the reason why Robert Plant has turned away from the song, declaring it a great song written at the right time for all the

right reasons, but now sanctimonious in the extreme. Free from the burden of having to interpret the lyrics, Jimmy Page remains justly proud of the composition, happy to celebrate its legacy as an instrumental live showpiece.

On the 20th anniversary of the original release of this song, it was announced via US radio sources that the song had logged up an estimated 2,874,000 radio plays – back to back that would run for 44 years solid. Its reverence in America remains unparalleled. In the UK there was a strong lobby from both Warners and Radio One to see the track issued as a single for the Christmas market in 1990. Ultimately – and unsurprisingly – the idea was vetoed. Rare original seven inch promos pressed at the time, accompanied by a humorous in-house memo (Atlantic LZ3), are amongst the most sought after UK rarities.

When they sat around that log fire all those years ago, they certainly could never have envisaged the impact 'Stairway To Heaven' would have on their career, that the song would become the single most requested track on American FM radio for most of the Seventies, or that it would inspire a whole album of cover versions.

Live performances: *Premièred at the Ulster Hall, Belfast, on March 5, 1971. Performed at every gig thereafter. Became the finale of the set from Rotterdam in 1975 to Berlin in 1980. Post-Zeppelin airings include the Live Aid and Atlantic reunions, plus instrumental versions by Page on the ARMS shows in 1983 and the 'Outrider' tour in 1988.*

MISTY MOUNTAIN HOP
PAGE, PLANT, JONES
STUDIOS: HEADLEY GRANGE WITH THE ROLLING STONES' MOBILE; OLYMPIC, LONDON

A happy up-tempo outing, written and recorded at the Grange, with Jones on electric piano. This is certainly a vintage Zeppelin song of which Plant has not grown tired. He has been more than happy to roll out its nostalgic hippy ideals during the Eighties, both on his solo tours, and at reunions with Page and Jones.

Live performances: *Joined the set on the European tour in 1971. Used as a link track for 'Since I've Been Loving You' from the Japan tour in 1972 up to the US tour in 1973. Dropped from the set then, but did reappear*

at the Copenhagen/Knebworth dates. Post-Zeppelin, it has been played by Plant on his solo tours, with Page at the Atlantic reunion, on a guest spot at Hammersmith in 1988, and at the Knebworth Silver Clef show in 1990.

FOUR STICKS
PAGE, PLANT
STUDIOS: ISLAND; OLYMPIC

A difficult track to record, this required many more takes than usual, and is so called because Bonzo employed the use of four drum sticks to create the relentless rhythm track. This was one of the tracks they recut with members of the Bombay Symphony Orchestra in 1972. It also features Jones on Moog synthesiser.

Live performance: *Only documented live performance is on the 1971 European tour in Copenhagen.*

GOING TO CALIFORNIA
PAGE, PLANT
STUDIOS: HEADLEY GRANGE WITH THE ROLLING STONES' MOBILE; OLYMPIC

Another acoustic beauty with some memorable Plant lyrics, heavily influenced by Joni Mitchell. This started out life as a song about Californian earthquakes and when Jimmy, Andy Johns and Peter Grant travelled to LA to mix the album, lo and behold the mountains did begin to tremble and shake. Then it was known as 'Guide To California'. It also tells of an unrequited search for the ultimate lady. 'It's infinitely hard,' Plant would often ad lib in the live rendition. Some 20 years later he gave an indication that his own search was ongoing, stating, 'Do you know what – it's still hard…' during the Knebworth 1990 show.

Live performances: *Introduced on the spring UK tour in 1971. Retained for all shows up to the next year's US tour. Returned to the set for Earls Court, and the 1977 US tour. Performed on Plant's solo tours during 1988/89 and at the Knebworth Silver Clef show in 1990.*

WHEN THE LEVEE BREAKS
PAGE, PLANT, JONES, BONHAM, MINNIE.
STUDIOS: HEADLEY GRANGE HAMPSHIRE WITH
THE ROLLING STONES' MOBILE;
SUNSET SOUND, LOS ANGELES

On June 18, 1929, in New York, Memphis Minnie and Kansas Joe McCoy recorded a blues tune called 'When The Levee Breaks'. Forty years later in leafy Hampshire, Led Zeppelin reconstructed the song to form the spiralling finale of their fourth album. It had already been tried unsuccessfully at Island at the beginning of the sessions but in Headley Grange it took on a whole new direction.

'Levee' goes down in the annals of Zeppelin history for Bonzo's crushing drum sound performed, according to Page, on a brand new kit that had only just been delivered from the factory. Engineer Andy Johns has revealed that the unique drum sound came about after Bonzo complained that he wasn't getting the sound he wanted. Johns promptly repositioned the kit in the Headley Grange hallway and hung two M1160 mikes from the staircase. Back in the Stones mobile he compressed the drum sound through two channels and added echo through Jimmy's Binson echo unit. The result was the most sampled and envied drum track in rock history.

Alongside that drum sound, Page contributes a rampant bottleneck guitar, while Plant blows a mean mouth harp that cleverly winds it all up in a barrage of backwards echo.

Live performances: *Rehearsed for the 1975 tour itinerary, it was tried out at the Rotterdam and Brussels warm up dates, but survived only a handful of opening shows on the subsequent US tour before being discarded.*

HOUSES OF THE HOLY

ATLANTIC RECORDS

K50014

Much of Led Zeppelin's fifth album was recorded at Stargroves, Mick Jagger's country estate in Berkshire, in the spring of 1972. Both Jimmy and John Paul had by now installed home studios of their own, enabling them to demo their own songs, and Jimmy was therefore able to present complete arrangements of 'The Rain Song' with its strange tunings and chiaroscuro dynamics, and another guitar extravaganza then known as 'Over The Hills'. Jones, meanwhile, had honed 'No Quarter', a track first tried out earlier at Headley Grange, into a brooding, quivering, synth-styled mantra.

Once installed in Stargroves other songs came from rehearsing together. These sessions on location, together with a further bout of recording at Olympic in May, proved so productive that some numbers didn't even make the final 'Houses Of The Holy' line-up. 'Black Country Woman', 'Walter's Walk', 'The Rover' and even the title track would all appear on later Led Zeppelin albums.

Following the overdubbing sessions at Olympic, Zeppelin commenced another extensive American tour. Along the way Eddie Kramer booked more time at Electric Lady studios in New York where Jimi Hendrix had once held court. It's rumoured that during these sessions the group committed to tape a series of rock'n'roll classics, including most of the tracks on 'Elvis' Gold Records Volume I' which they liked to play at sound checks before concerts.

It's been suggested that Jimmy wasn't as happy with the overall sound from Stargroves compared to that at Headley Grange. This I find surprising. There's a confidence and maturity about the 'Houses' album that accounted for a notable progression in their ensemble playing. "I can remember Bonzo, Plant, Page and Jones out on the lawn listening to playbacks of 'D'yer Mak'er' and 'Dancing Days' all walking like Groucho Marx in sync, with back steps and forward steps in time to the music," recalls Eddie Kramer and these tracks in particular vividly illustrated the good to be alive feel of the period.

'Houses Of The Holy' ushered in the golden middle period of Zeppelin supremacy. By the time of its release on March 26, 1973, Led Zeppelin were unquestionably the most popular live band in America and probably the world. Along with The Rolling Stones and The Who, they formed a mighty triumvirate of great British bands who bestrode the rock concert industry like colossi.

After the usual long delay due to the inevitable sleeve problems, 'Houses' tied in nicely with a tour of Europe that was closely followed with a two-legged assault on America. In fact the week the album ascended to the top of the American chart, Led Zeppelin opened their US tour by playing two mammoth dates. In Atlanta they drew 49,000 on May 4, while the next day a staggering 56,800 packed into the Tampa stadium in Florida. This gave them the distinction of attracting the largest audience ever for a single act perfor-

mance, beating the previous record held by The Beatles for their Shea Stadium show. It was a record that they themselves would top at the Silverdome Pontiac four years later.

'Houses Of The Holy' had been recorded almost a year previously, and much of the material had been tested on audiences across the US, Japan, UK and Europe during 1972/3. It was first touted for release early in January, when it was known as 'Led Zeppelin V'. The delays came with the sleeve. This time they chose a collage print depicting a group of children mysteriously scaling the top of a mountain, which, according to Page, denoted the feeling of expectancy for the music contained within.

The distinctive sleeve design was the product of a meeting between the Hipgnosis sleeve design team and Jimmy, Robert and Peter Grant. Aubrey Powell of Hipgnosis recalls that both Peru and Ireland were considered for location shooting, with the Giant's Causeway in Ireland eventually being chosen. Powell took two children along and based his image on a science fiction book called *Childhood's End*.

The outer photos were shot in black and

white in appalling conditions while the inner sleeve was taken at a nearby castle. All the shots were later airbrushed, though original instructions for the children to be gold and silver were amended by accident to a more atmospheric purple. The shots with the two children were multi-printed to create the effect of 11 nubiles that adorned the finished article.

This elaborate printing technique delayed the original January 5 release date to late

March. Following in the tradition of the fourth album, it was an artistic statement that gave little indication of the musical content within. This, of course, only added to Led Zeppelin's increasing mystique. Given the minimal approach of modern day CD packaging, the 'Houses' sleeve remains a shining example of the gloriously self indulgent nature of Seventies album cover artwork.

After the furore of the wordless fourth album, Grant did allow Atlantic to add a wrap-around band to UK copies of the sleeve. Surprisingly, this tactic survived well into the Eighties. However, the CD version does have the title logos printed on the cover itself, a further indication of the lack of quality control applied when the original CDs were issued.

Despite receiving some decidedly mixed reviews, the album entered the UK chart at number one, while in America its 39-week run on the *Billboard* Top 40 was their longest since the first album.

Much of the press criticism was levelled at the tongue in cheek nature of tracks such as 'The Crunge' and 'D'yer Mak'er'. Once again they had not travelled down the expected path, and in pleasing themselves they may have not pleased the critics. But their ever increasing following, as the 1973 US tour testified, was still with them every step of the way. In retrospect, 'Houses Of The Holy' holds its ground with the middle period releases quite admirably. The barnstorming effect of the early era was now levelling off and though devoid of the electricity of 'Zeppelin I' and 'II', or the sheer diversity of the third album, and lacking the classic status of the fourth, 'Houses' took stock of their situation. In doing so, it laid several foundations on which they would expand their future collective musical aspirations.

THE SONG REMAINS THE SAME
PAGE, PLANT
STUDIOS: STARGROVES, BERKSHIRE, WITH THE ROLLING STONES' MOBILE; OLYMPIC, LONDON

This shimmering Page extravaganza was originally conceived as an instrumental known as 'The Overture'. When Plant added the lyrics, it took on the working title of 'The Campaign'. The finished article is an uplifting barrage of six-stringed picking and chording, over which Plant's slightly speeded-up vocal track chronicles their travels and observes that the common denominator to it all is that if you give, you get back, in fact 'The Song Remains The Same'. Another track that Jimmy transferred to the Gibson doubleneck to play live, in the studio he overdubs on Telecaster, and a Rickenbacker 12-string. John Paul Jones also puts in some wonderful bass lines.

Live performances: *Premièred on the Japanese tour in October 1972. Retained for every live gig up to Earls Court in 1975. This arrangement always dove-tailed into its studio counterpart 'The Rain Song'. From the US tour in 1977 up to the 1979 Copenhagen and Knebworth shows, the track was employed as a suitably vibrant set opener in its own right. It was then rested for the Europe dates.*

THE RAIN SONG
PAGE, PLANT
STUDIOS: STARGROVES WITH
THE ROLLING STONES' MOBILE: OLYMPIC

This was one of the new songs for 'Houses' that benefited from the recent installation of a studio console at Jimmy's Plumpton home. A new Vista model, it was partly made up from the Pye Mobile Studio which had been used to record the group's 1970 Albert Hall show and The Who's 'Live At Leeds' album.

Page was able to bring in a completed arrangement of the melody for which Robert matched some sensitive lyrics. This track also marks the début of the John Paul Jones one-man orchestra. He layers on a drifting string symphony created by a mellotron, an early sampling keyboard synth. Page plays his Dan Electro guitar here. The working title for this song was 'Slush', a reference to its easy listening mock orchestral arrangement.

Live performances: *Came into the set as a dual performance with 'The Song Remains The Same'. Retained in this format on every subsequent tour up to Earls Court in 1975. When 'The Song' became the set opener, 'The Rain Song' was dropped for the 1977 dates. However, it was revived as a solo piece for the Copenhagen, Knebworth and Europe 1979/80 gigs. Another number which required the Gibson double-neck guitar on stage.*

OVER THE HILLS AND FAR AWAY
PAGE, PLANT
STUDIOS: STARGROVES WITH THE ROLLING STONES'
MOBILE; ELECTRIC LADY

Opens with some superbly interwoven acoustic playing, before shifting gear for an electric chorus that finds the Jones/Bonham rhythm bond steadfast as ever. Plant meanwhile waxes hippily about that open road (and that Acapulco gold). A cut that displays all the colour and light of the group's maturing musical landscape.

Archive footage of this track being performed live at Seattle in 1977 and Knebworth in 1979 was used for an officially distributed video of the song used to promote the 1990 'Remasters' releases.

Live performances: *One of the new songs to be introduced on stage way ahead of the album's release. This track came in on the 1972 US trip. Usually employed in the early part of the set to provide Page with a chance to warm up the Gibson, it stayed with them for each tour up to the Copenhagen/Knebworth shows in 1979. Performed by Jimmy on his solo 'Outrider' tour in 1988.*

THE CRUNGE
BONHAM, JONES, PAGE, PLANT
STUDIOS: STARGROVES WITH THE ROLLING STONES'
MOBILE; OLYMPIC; ELECTRIC LADY

'The Crunge' came out of a Bonham inspired spontaneous jam at Stargroves. Jimmy came in with a funk riff (and a chord sequence he'd had kicking around since 1970), stepping on and off the beat, rendering the whole thing completely undanceable. This spurred Robert to come up with a set of lyrics that parodied the James Brown/'Take it to the bridge' school of funk mannerisms. With tongue firmly planted in cheek, they named this non-dance cult 'The Crunge' and even thought about illustrating the 'dance steps' on the cover. Maybe the critics would then have seen the joke. Incidentally, that's Jimmy and engineer George Chkianz you can hear talking, just as Bonzo comes in on the intro.

Live performances: *Never performed as a track in its own right, 'The Crunge' was incorporated firstly during 'Dazed And Confused' on the 1972 US tour, and more commonly within 'Whole Lotta Love' up to the 1975 dates. It was mainly put in as an ad libbed* *instrumental though on occasions did receive a full Plant vocal, notably on the March 24/25 1975 LA Forum dates where on the latter night it was sequenced together with James Brown's 'Sex Machine'. A bootleg from this gig was entitled 'Sex Machine And The Butter Queen'!*

DANCING DAYS
PAGE, PLANT
STUDIOS: STARGROVES WITH THE ROLLING STONES'
MOBILE: ELECTRIC LADY

Built around another classically incessant Page riff, this is a complete joy from start to finish. Plant captures the intended 'good to be alive' vibe with a smiling vocal, as he sings about those lazy hazy summer nights. It comes as no surprise to hear Eddie Kramer's story of them dancing out on the Stargroves lawn during the playback of this track. It summarises the positive atmosphere of the time perfectly.

This was the first track from the album to be offered for radio play by Atlantic. It was premièred on Saturday March 24, 1973, on the Radio One Rosko lunch time show.

Live performances: *First aired as early as the first 'Electric Magic' gig at the Wembley Empire Pool on November 20, 1971, it re-emerged during the second half of the 1972 US tour and at the Seattle Coliseum on June 19 when it was played twice: first in the main set, then as an encore! Discarded for the '73 US tour, it made a surprise on the '77 US tour, this time as part of the acoustic medley with 'Bron-Y-Aur Stomp'. A complete acoustic version was also performed at the June 27 Forum show in 1977.*

D'YER MAK'ER
BONHAM, JONES, PAGE, PLANT
STUDIOS: STARGROVES WITH THE ROLLING STONES'
MOBILE: ELECTRIC LADY

Another number constructed out of rehearsals at Stargroves. Bonzo came up with the song's structure, which set out to capture a Fifties do-wop feel (hence the Rosie And The Originals sleeve credit) and what began as a mock Fifties spoof *à la* Ben E. King then twisted into a reggae off beat. By retaining this slight off-beat on the tempo, the subtle reggae influence emerged, which the critics were quick to jump on. Such was the commercial appeal of this track, Robert Plant was supremely keen to issue it as a single in the UK. Atlantic even went as far as distributing advance promo copies to DJ's, but the others did not share Plant's enthusiasm for its release. The promo copies have become much sought after Zeppelin collectables. 'D'Yer Mak'er' remained on the album only, its old English music hall joke title destined to confuse our American cousins, while the music profiled Bonzo at his very best.

'D'Yer Mak'er' seems to have become a controversial issue within the band. Jones has asserted his disdain for the number, feeling it started off as a joke and wasn't thought through carefully enough.

Live performances: *Though never performed live in its entirety, Plant did throw in lines from the song during the 'Whole Lotta Love' medley circa 1973/75, notably at the March 21 date in Hamburg on the 1973 European tour.*

NO QUARTER
JONES, PAGE, PLANT

STUDIOS: STARGROVES WITH THE ROLLING STONES' MOBILE; OLYMPIC; ELECTRIC LADY

This brooding Jones creation had been tried a year earlier at Headley Grange. Now slowed down in tempo, and with added synth, bass and piano effects, it took on a dark mysterious texture. Plant's vocals are superbly treated, while the instrumental passage, where Jones' grand piano merges with Page and Bonham's understated rhythmic touches, is a sequence of high drama and quite breathtaking in its delivery.

One of their foremost studio achievements, outtake versions that have emerged on the bootleg CD 'Studio Daze' offer much insight into the song's construction and again demonstrate Bonzo's vital contribution to the feel of the track. On the instrumental backing track outtakes he lays down exquisite spacey snare fills for Jimmy and Jonesy to work around. The guitar solo effect was achieved by direct injunction and compression.

Live performances: *Not surprisingly this particular journey became a centrepiece of their*

live shows. Thus from its introduction to the set on the 1973 US tour, it developed into a marathon Jones showcase, played at every show through to Knebworth in 1979. At the LA Forum on March 25, 1975, Page, Jones and Bonham took the song into a very atypical jazz arrangement quite unlike any other version in that era, and during 1977 live versions of the song included a full version of B. Bumble And The Stingers' 'Nut Rocker'. It was deleted from the set on the scaled down Europe shows of 1980. Plant reintroduced the number to his 'Manic Nirvana' tour in 1990. The arrangement on this occasion, however, did not remain the same.

THE OCEAN
BONHAM, JONES, PAGE, PLANT
STUDIOS: STARGROVES WITH THE ROLLING STONES'
MOBILE; OLYMPIC; ELECTRIC LADY

'We've done four already but now we're steady and then they went... ' John Bonham's thick Midlands accent rings in this delightful closing rocker. Just as the title of the song had been a Plant metaphor for the sea of heads he faced in the auditoriums they were now filling,

'The Ocean' refers to Zeppelin's ever growing and ever faithful army of fans. 'Has the ocean lost its way, I don't think so', he reflects, going on to explain his devotion to baby Carmen ('she is only three-years old').

Page and Co meanwhile strut out another memorable riff that would later inspire a few thousand sales of Beastie Boys albums. The closing do-wop finale is a further joy. 'So good!' shouts Plant and he's so right.

Live performances: *This high energy outing came into the set as early as the 1972 summer tour. It was an encore during the UK tour dates of 1973. It was further employed on the European trek in the spring, and the summer tour of the US. Deleted thereafter. During Plant's solo tours samples of the track and the 'la-la-la-la-la-la' chorus were inserted into 'Tall Cool One'. Page quoted from the song's riff during his live version of 'Custard Pie' on the 1988 Outrider tour.*

PHYSICAL GRAFFITI

SWAN SONG

SSK 89400

For their inaugural Swan Song release, Led Zeppelin finally succumbed to the double album format. A combination of new material recorded early in 1974 at Headley Grange, coupled with a summary of strong material from previous sessions, made up the contents of this blockbuster release.

After the hugely successful 1973 American tour, Led Zeppelin unwound, did some home movie work for their film, and took their time approaching their next recording sessions. It wasn't until November that they returned to Headley Grange with Ronnie Lane's mobile studio for location recording, but the sessions came to a halt fairly quickly and the time was given over to Bad Company who were also managed by Peter Grant. At the time the reason given was that John Paul Jones was ill, but it later emerged that Jones had wanted to quit the band to take up a position as choirmaster at Winchester Cathedral. Peter Grant urged caution, suggesting that Jones was overwrought from the incessant touring and should take a rest from Zeppelin for a few weeks. Jones changed his mind and sessions resumed at Headley Grange after the Christmas holidays.

Once re-united, it was a case of pooling ideas. Mostly what they had were, as Robert later described them, 'the belters'. "We got eight tracks off," he explained in the spring of 1974, "and a lot of them are really raunchy. We did some real belters with live vocals, off-the-wall stuff that turned out really nice."

Similar to the sessions for the previous two albums, the location recording technique gave them ample time to develop material along the way. Plant again: "Some of the tracks we assembled in our own fashioned way of running through a track and realising before we knew it that we had stumbled on something

completely different."

A distinct character of these sessions is the throatiness of Robert's vocals. Talking to *The Scotsman* newspaper in 1988, Plant said: "Fifteen years ago I had an operation on my throat and couldn't speak for three weeks." If

Robert had got his dates right, the period he was talking about was the autumn/winter of 1973/4, and this may explain why his voice was less than crystal clear for the sixth album sessions.

Those eight tracks, engineered by Ron Nevison, extended beyond the length of a conventional album and this prompted them to construct a double set. This was achieved by reassessing the material recorded for earlier albums, from which seven further tracks were added. The whole package was mixed down by the late Keith Harwood at Olympic, and released as 'Physical Graffiti' in 1975. It was a massive outpouring of Zeppelin music that proved to be the definitive summary of their studio work.

The sleeve design is one of their most elaborate. The front cover depicts a New York tenement block (actual location: 96 St. Marks, NYC), through which interchanging window illustrations reveal such candid shots as the group dressed in drag, and Bonzo in tights for the Roy Harper St. Valentine's Day gig.

The title 'Physical Graffiti' was coined by Page to illustrate the whole physical and written energy that had gone into producing the set. The release date was timed to coincide with their 1975 tour campaign which commenced in America in January. Minor delays kept it from appearing until late February. When it did appear the demand was staggering.

'Physical Graffiti' made what had by now become Led Zeppelin's customary entry at number one on the UK chart, while America just went 'Graffiti' mad. It entered every US chart at number three, then a record for a new entry, before lodging itself at the top for six weeks. Even more remarkable was the fact all five previous Zepp albums returned to the *Billboard* chart. No other rock act had ever been so well represented.

It had been two years since their last album, but the waiting had been worth it. Led Zeppelin had delivered. It still stands as their finest recorded achievement. Given the luxury of the double format, 'Physical Graffiti' mirrors every facet of the Zeppelin repertoire. The end result is a finely balanced embarrassment of riches. Through light and shade, from a whisper to a scream, this one has it all.

CUSTARD PIE
PAGE, PLANT
STUDIOS: HEADLEY GRANGE WITH
RONNIE LANE'S MOBILE; OLYMPIC

One of the belters from Headley Grange, 'Custard Pie' is a prime knockabout rocker with a vintage Page riff, finely undercut by J.P. on clavinet. As well as tapping the Bukka

White songbook for the 'shake 'em on down' refrain, other sources of inspiration can be traced to Sonny Boy Fuller's 'Custard Pie Blues', Blind Boy Fuller's 'I Want Some Of Your Custard Pie' and Big Joe Williams' version of the song, 'Drop Down Mama'. Plant throws in a bluesy mouth harp to aid the effect, Page filters a piercing solo through an ARP synthesiser, and it all dances off to a pleasing fade. 'Drop down!' squeals Plant and Bonzo duly obliges with a typically robust attack on the bass drum.

Live performances: *Although rehearsed for the 1975 set, 'Custard Pie' never received a public Zeppelin airing. Years later, Plant would redress the balance by incorporating a chorus of the song on the end of the live version of 'Tall Cool One'. Page also produced his own live version on the 'Outrider' tour during the same year. It was also performed at the Jason Bonham wedding reunion in 1990.*

THE ROVER
PAGE, PLANT
STUDIOS: STARGROVES, BERKSHIRE, WITH THE ROLLING STONES' MOBILE; OLYMPIC

A track that dates back to 1970, 'The Rover' was rehearsed as an acoustic blues piece before being recorded at Stargroves with Eddie Kramer for the fifth album. When it didn't make the final 'Houses Of The Holy' selection, Page returned to it in 1974, overdubbing and re-mixing the basic track with Keith Harwood. The curious 'Guitar lost courtesy Nevison… Salvaged by the grace of Harwood' sleeve credit would appear to be a reference to certain mixing difficulties they may have had here – Nevison being engineer Ron Nevison.

'The Rover' possesses a stirring melodic base, from which Plant waxes idealistically about the need for solidarity, and Page strings together one of his most perfectly constructed solos.

Live performances: *Though elements of the song were heard on stage during 1972 and 1977, no complete version was ever played. However, the song was rehearsed in full, as can be heard on the remarkable soundcheck* rehearsal tape recorded on July 6 at the Chicago Auditorium and now available on the bootleg CDs 'Round And Round' and 'Tribute To Johnny Kidd And The Pirates'. The rehearsal took place before the opening date of the second half of the tour. "In those days we used to play songs that were totally unrelated to the current tour during rehearsals. In fact, loads of songs were born in the rehearsal jam session," Page said in 1990.

IN MY TIME OF DYING
BONHAM, JONES, PAGE, PLANT
STUDIOS: HEADLEY GRANGE WITH
RONNIE LANE'S MOBILE, OLYMPIC

A traditional song that can be found on Bob Dylan's first album, Zeppelin's arrangement came together during the initial sixth album sessions in 1974. The lyrics can be traced back to a 1927 recording by Blind Willie Johnson entitled 'Jesus Make Up My Dying Bed'. With one of the most powerful drum sounds ever committed to tape (recorded in the same way as 'When The Levee Breaks'), the point where Page straps in for a peerless bottleneck frenzy backed by Jonesy and

Bonzo at the nerve centre, has to be one of the most scintillating moments in the whole of the Zeppelin catalogue. The intensity is quite frightening. It eventually winds down via a studio cough from Bonzo. "That's gotta be the one hasn't it?" enquires the drummer from behind the screens. Indeed it was . . .

Live performances: *Brought in to the revamped set for all their 1975 dates and used again on some of the 1977 US tour where it was alternated with 'Over The Hills And Far Away'. It was a number that Plant was unsure of performing after his 1975 car crash, due to its fatalistic lyrical theme. Also performed by Page on his solo 'Outrider' tour.*

HOUSES OF THE HOLY
PAGE, PLANT
STUDIOS: OLYMPIC; ELECTRIC LADY

Another fifth album overspill, this title track was recalled for the double set and required no further re-mixing, having been tied up by Eddie Kramer as far back as the Electric Lady sessions in June 1972. A strident mid-tempo exercise with the same smiling friendliness in its grooves as can be heard on 'Dancing Days'. This similarity may have accounted for its absence on the 'Houses Of The Holy' album. In order to create the layered guitar intro and fade, Jimmy used a Delta T digital delay unit.

Live performances: *Never performed live.*

TRAMPLED UNDERFOOT
JONES, PAGE, PLANT
STUDIOS: HEADLEY GRANGE WITH
RONNIE LANE'S MOBILE; OLYMPIC

Much rehearsal went into perfecting the relentless semi-funk riff that dominates this driving tale of the motor car and its relation with the sexual act, a theme explored by Robert Johnson in 'Terraplane Blues'. Jones' clavinet and Jimmy's wah-wah and backwards echo make for a formidable partnership. Plant's vocals are a little too back in the mix (a characteristic of most of the Headley Grange tracks) but not enough to dim the overall incessant effect, which remains quite irresistible. Special UK singles of this track were pressed for promotional purposes in time for the Earls Court shows.

Live performances: *Another Zeppelin concert showpiece, this track was played on every live show from 1975 through to the last gig in Berlin in 1980. For some of the 1977 US shows it became an encore number. In 1988 it was revived by Plant for his 'Now And Zen' tour, including a memorable performance with Jimmy at Hammersmith in April.*

KASHMIR
BONHAM, PAGE, PLANT
STUDIOS: HEADLEY GRANGE WITH
RONNIE LANE'S MOBILE; OLYMPIC

This particular epic grew out of two separate Page riffs which he was unable to combine until he and John Bonham demoed it late in 1973. Robert wrote the lyrics on the road to Tan Tan while holidaying in South Morocco immediately after the 1973 US tour, and called it 'Driving To Kashmir' as a working title. He was later to refer to it as 'The Pride of Led Zeppelin'.

When it came to recording in early 1974, J.P. scored a suitable Eastern string arrangement. Kashmir's real beauty of course, lies in Page's Moorish chord riff that carries the song towards those desert wastelands. There is an ethereal, slightly discordant and somewhat eerie quality to this music that hints at the mysteries of the East and seems derived from musical signatures not normally found in the standard Western scale. Page has revealed that outside session musicians were brought in to add strings and horns, a rare occurrence on a Zeppelin session.

Unquestionably the most startling and impressive track on 'Physical Graffiti', and arguably the most progressive and original track that Led Zeppelin ever recorded, 'Kashmir' went a long way towards establishing their credibility with otherwise sceptical rock critics. Many would regard this track as the finest example of the sheer majesty of Zeppelin's special chemistry.

Live performances: *Made its début in Rotterdam on January 11, 1975. Performed on every subsequent gig up to the final show in Berlin on July 7, 1980. From the 1977 US dates onwards, 'Kashmir' led out of Jimmy's 'White Summer'/'Black Mountain Side' solo guitar spot, for which he switched to playing a Dan Electro guitar. Post-Zeppelin, it was aired at the Atlantic Records 21st birthday celebrations at Madison Square Garden. Jimmy also slotted in a few riffs of this epic during the 'Moonlight Midnight' medley on his 'Outrider' tour.*

IN THE LIGHT
JONES, PAGE, PLANT
STUDIOS: HEADLEY GRANGE WITH RONNIE LANE'S MOBILE; OLYMPIC

'In The Light' grew out of a similar-styled rehearsal number known as 'In The Morning'. Opening with a drone-like keyboard effect from Jones, the track travels down more than one tempo change, as Robert sings with great passion about the need for eternal optimism. The fade-out is another wonderful example of the interplay enjoyed by Jimmy and Bonzo, as a mass of overdubbed guitar parts filter round some exemplary percussion. More than enough reason for Jimmy to select this number as his favourite track on the whole album.

Live performances: *Surprisingly enough, this was never attempted live. It was, however, used as an intro link to 'Nobody's Fault But Mine' on some of Plant's 'Now And*

Zen' American shows in 1988. If 'The 80s Part One' tour had occurred, this would have been a perfect vehicle for Jonesey's 'Dream Machine'.

BRON-Y-AUR
PAGE
STUDIOS: ISLAND, LONDON; OLYMPIC

A short winsome acoustic solo, written and tried for 'Zeppelin III'. Later to appear as part of the non-performance soundtrack to *The Song Remains The Same* movie.

Live performances: *Briefly part of the acoustic set on the sixth American tour August/September 1970.*

DOWN BY THE SEASIDE
PAGE, PLANT
STUDIOS: ISLAND; OLYMPIC

Another song written at Bron-Y-Aur in the Spring of 1970. Originally conceived as a Neil Young-influenced acoustic strum-along (with Robert playing guitar), this electric arrangement was recorded at the time of the fourth

album sessions. It features some lively electric piano, a sensitive Plant vocal, and an unexpected rise in tempo half way through. The manner in which Page and Bonham turn away from the tranquil landscape of the song to take it all up a gear, and then slip back to the original lilting theme with effortless ease, is a master-stroke of controlled dynamics.

Live performances: *Never performed live.*

TEN YEARS GONE
PAGE, PLANT
STUDIOS: HEADLEY GRANGE WITH RONNIE LANE'S MOBILE; OLYMPIC

Originally a Page instrumental and quite possibly a variation of the often mentioned but never released Led Zeppelin track 'Swan Song' (the name they chose for their own record label). A moving Plant narrative about an age old love affair that still cuts deep. The emotional content of this piece is further emphasised by the subtle Page embellishments that colour the song. A series of overdubbed guitar parts, all in perfect harmony, hint at the original intention of this track being an instrumental tour-de-force. As it turned out, it stands as one of their finest arrangements.

Live performances: *Brought in for the 1977 US tour. JP originally played the melody on acoustic guitar but then introduced a special three-necked guitar that encompassed bass pedals, mandolin and six- and 12-string acoustics. Played again on the July 24 Copenhagen warm-up show and at the August 4 Knebworth show in 1979. The problems encountered in setting up Jones' multi-faceted instrument probably accounted for its omission at the following week's concert and at the other Copenhagen warm-up.*

NIGHT FLIGHT
JONES, PAGE, PLANT
STUDIOS: HEADLEY GRANGE WITH THE ROLLING
STONES' MOBILE; OLYMPIC; ISLAND

A bright rollercoaster rocker from the sessions at Headley Grange for the fourth album. Robert and Bonzo are on dazzling form here. Plant's strident vocals are crystal clear and supported by some turbulent drumming. Page, meanwhile, puts in some swirling Leslie

guitar, playing off a warm organ sound supplied by J.P. An outtake with extra backing vocals on the middle eight section remains in the vaults.

Live performances: *Although never played live, it can be heard in a rehearsal version from the July 6 1973 Chicago soundcheck, an arrangement that testifies to its 1971 vintage.*

THE WANTON SONG
PAGE, PLANT
STUDIOS: HEADLEY GRANGE WITH
RONNIE LANE'S MOBILE; OLYMPIC

'The Wanton Song' is a thrusting Plant tale of carnal delights, ably supported by a devastatingly simple but quite brilliant Page riff that grinds the listener into submission. His guitar effects include the use of backwards echo during the solo and refrain, and also playing through a Leslie speaker to create the organ effect. Jones and Bonham back up with a barrage of noise with equal panache. A reassuringly tough product of the sixth album sessions in 1974.

Live performances: *The bridge of the song is another piece of Zeppelin music that can be heard clearly on the Chicago July 6 soundcheck tape. It was played on the European warm up dates in early 1975 and some of the opening 1975 US tour dates and then discarded.*

BOOGIE WITH STU
BONHAM, JONES, PAGE, PLANT, STEWART, MRS VALENS
STUDIOS: HEADLEY GRANGE WITH THE ROLLING
STONES' MOBILE; OLYMPIC

A loose jam recorded at the same sessions which produced 'Rock And Roll' for the fourth album. This has Ian Stewart, The Rolling Stones' tour manager and resident boogie-woogie keyboard player, playing barrel-house piano. Heavily based on Richie Valens' Fifties hit 'Ooh My Head' (check out the *La Bamba* movie), hence the credit to his widow. The slapping guitar came from an overdub session with the ARP guitar synth. Robert came up with the working title 'Sloppy Drunk'.

Live performances: *Never performed live.*

BLACK COUNTRY WOMAN
PAGE, PLANT
STUDIOS: THE GARDEN AT STARGROVES WITH THE
ROLLING STONES' MOBILE; OLYMPIC

Ever on the look-out for off-the-wall recording locations (Plant once tried to record some vocals out in the quadrangle of Headley Grange and had to flee from a gaggle of geese that attacked him!), the boys took to the garden at Stargroves for this session in the spring of 1972. The resulting take was nearly shelved when a plane cruised overhead, but as the opening dialogue reveals, it was all captured for posterity. Prior to release 'Black Country Woman' was sub-titled 'Never Ending Doubting Woman Blues'. This was a reference to a final spoken tag left off the finished version which had Robert proclaiming, 'What's the matter with you mama, never-ending, nagging, doubting woman blues.'

Live performances: *This was performed at one show at least in America in 1972. It was then merged into a medley with 'Bron-Y-Aur Stomp' for the 1977 US dates. Revived by Plant on his 1988 Now And Zen tour.*

SICK AGAIN
PAGE, PLANT
STUDIOS: HEADLEY GRANGE WITH
RONNIE LANE'S MOBILE; OLYMPIC

And finally… a mid tempo-rocker based on Plant's still vivid tales of the 1973 US tour and the ladies that surrounded them. It's powered by a series of Page runs and some ferocious Bonham hammering that assist in conjuring up the required images. Juicy and muscular and inevitably tight but loose, 'Sick Again' is a fitting exit. Listen carefully and you can hear Bonzo coughing out loud after Page's sonic finale.

Live performances: *Held the distinction of being the second number performed on all the 1975 and 1977 tour dates. On the 1977 tour it was preceded by a link from 'The Rover'. It was rehearsed at Bray Studios during the summer of 1979 for its return to the set but it only made three out of the four 79 shows. It's likely it was exorcised from the first Copenhagen show due to the late running because of a power failure.*

PRESENCE

SWAN SONG

SSK 59402

And suddenly there was 'Presence'. Forced by Robert Plant's car smash to cancel a projected world tour due to commence on August 23, 1975, the group wisely used this period of convalescence to write and record a new album.

The seeds of this album can be traced back to when Page joined Plant recuperating in Malibu (which explains why most of the album consists solely of Page/Plant compositions). Robert had already written some reflective lyrics and coupled with Page's input, these fragments of songs were soon under rehearsal as Jones and Bonham flew over for pre-production sessions at Hollywood's SIR rehearsal studios. After a month of rehearsals, the group were anxious to record. Musicland studios in Munich (a favourite Page haunt) was their next destination. In the fastest time since the first album, seven tracks were laid down in a period of just three weeks.

"I think it was just a reflection of the total anxiety and emotion of the period," Page said at the time. "There's a hell of a lot of spontaneity about that album. We went in with virtually nothing and everything just came pouring out."

With his partner at less than full fitness, Page took total responsibility for the album's completion. His playing and production dominate the album's seven tracks, and in stark contrast to the relaxed atmosphere of the last four albums, this album came together through intense 18-hour-day sessions. In fact the studio time booked actually overran, forcing Page to borrow two days from the incoming Rolling Stones, during which time he completed the album's overdubs. (When Page politely requested the extra time from Mick Jagger, the venerable Stone was reportedly amazed that Zeppelin had put their album together so quickly and that Jimmy required only *two* extra days for overdubs. Rolling Stones albums, it seems, took many months to complete.)

The album was completed on November 27, the day before Thanksgiving. In a call to Swan Song the next day, an ecstatic Plant suggested the album be named 'Thanksgiving'. As it turned out, meetings with sleeve designers Hipgnosis dictated otherwise. Telling Page of the incredibly powerful force and presence they felt surrounded the group, he briefed them to come up with a sleeve that displayed this fact. The bizarre result, a series of *Life* magazine prints of everyday events, mostly involving conservative looking families from middle-America during the Fifties, interrupted by the 'presence' in the form of a mysterious black obelisk (The Object), confused both media and enthusiasts alike. At one stage the plan was to dub the album 'Obelisk'. Page held out for 'Presence'.

As ever, the sleeve caused delays and it was eventually released in early April 1976. The promotion for the album centred around The Object, the weird obelisk depicted on the cover. In Britain it attained one of the highest ever advance orders, shipping gold on the day of release. In America it leapt from 24 to number one inside two weeks.

Long term, 'Presence' was not one of Zeppelin's biggest sellers. Somewhat over-shadowed by the late 1976 release of their movie and soundtrack, it has become a much underrated element of their catalogue. The basic drums-bass-guitars formula may lack the diversity of previous Zeppelin sets, but in terms of sheer energy, 'Presence' packs a considerable punch, and has emerged as one of their most potent performances. It was the state-of-the-art multi-dubbing facility at the Musicland studio console that accounted for 'Achilles Last Stand', a major Zeppelin opus and a track that excited Plant so much during playback that he fell over and nearly reopened his wounds from the car crash in Greece.

This album is also a triumph for Jimmy Page. His production and dominant guitar style has an urgency and passion that reflects the troubled period that the group were going through at the time. 'Presence' is Led Zeppelin with their backs against the wall. As Page once put it, "We started screaming in rehearsals and never stopped."

ACHILLES LAST STAND
PAGE, PLANT
STUDIO: MUSICLAND, MUNICH

'Achilles Last Stand' is a glorious 10-minute opening salvo that finds all the musicians pushing their talents to the limit. John Bonham's drumming is at once both explosive and inventive, driven along by an irresistible chugging Jones bass line. All this acts as a perfect lynchpin for Page to weave his magic. His playing, constantly overdubbed, is simply magnificent, scaling the song's basic two pronged structure with amazing dexterity. Robert meanwhile unravels a bizarre tale inspired by his and Page's travels across Africa immediately after the Earls Court shows. With its theme of movement, meeting and positive outlook, his lyrics act as a perfect foil for the relentless pace of the track.

'Achilles Last Stand' is an absolutely crucial performance and one that remains as vital today as it did when it took shape inside Musicland back in 1975. A definitive Led Zeppelin yardstick.

Live performances: *The first number to be rehearsed when they regrouped in late 1976 for the 1977 US tour, 'Achilles' held its place in the set through 1977, Copenhagen and Knebworth 1979 and right up to the last night of the 'Over Europe' tour. Strangely, it was omitted from what was to be their final show in Berlin. Page expected to use the Gibson double-neck when it came to performing this epic live, but found it worked fine with just the Gibson Les Paul, or as employed at Knebworth 1, the red Telecaster.*

FOR YOUR LIFE
PAGE, PLANT
STUDIO: MUSICLAND

Much to admire here both lyrically and musically. Built on a grinding, penetrating riff, it finds Plant in understandably reflective mood. 'In the pits you go no lower, the next stop's underground', he observes, a phrase that hints at this composition's Malibu period origin. Much of the basic track was created inside Musicland. The cutting solo that Page plays marks the recorded début of a new part of his guitar arsenal – a 1962 Lake Placid blue

Fender Stratocaster (supplied by ex-Byrd Gene Parsons), later to be employed on stage during 1979/80 and with The Firm. Not instantly appealing, 'For Your Life' seeps into the consciousness with repeated hearings.

Live performances: *Never performed live.*

ROYAL ORLEANS
BONHAM, JONES, PAGE, PLANT
STUDIO: MUSICLAND

Royal Orleans is the name of a hotel in New Orleans located at 621 St Louis Street which was often favoured by the group in their touring heyday and is the setting for this whimsical 'road fever' lament. It tells the tale of 'a man I know' (whose initials were rumoured to be J.P.J.) whose association with the local clientèle provided something of a surprise.

Listen carefully at the end for a great reference to that old soul-swayer Barry White. All this is played out against a short, sharp riff injection, from which Page throws in some funky lines and Bonzo takes to the bongos.

'Royal Orleans' 'road fever' lyrical content would suggest it was a composition that Plant had written some time previous to this period.

When the entire 'Presence' album was pre-mièred on the Alan Freeman show on Radio One on April 3, 1976, the version of this track had an edit in the middle of the solo. This could have been cut to accommodate radio timings, or perhaps this version was taken from an early mix of the album used for pre-release promotion.

Live performances: *Never performed live.*

wrote the lyrics back in 1928, a fact Robert acknowledged when introducing the track on stage in Copenhagen in 1979.

Live performances: *A welcome addition to the set on the 1977 US tour. It remained a stage favourite through to the Copenhagen, Knebworth and Europe dates in 1979/80. It was also revived by Plant for his solo tours in 1988 and 1990.*

NOBODY'S FAULT BUT MINE
PAGE, PLANT
STUDIO: MUSICLAND

A full-blooded blues/rock stomper that opens with some suitable sonic embellishments from Jimmy. The up front preening of Page and Plant are duly supported on the flanks by some steadfast rhythm work by J. P. and Bonzo, who handle the stop-go interludes with masterful restraint. Plant blows a mean harmonica before yet another stirring Page onslaught. All in all, a great throwback to some earlier blues-inspired performances. The Page/Plant credit here is a little misleading as Blind Willie Johnson may well have been under the impression that he

CANDY STORE ROCK
PAGE, PLANT
STUDIO: MUSICLAND

A basic Fifties-flavoured rock'n'roll groove strung along by some Scotty Moore guitar figures from Page. Heavily echoed Plant vocal in the style of Elvis impersonating Ral Donner, up front bass from J.P. and plenty of timpani in the percussion department add to a performance that years later Plant would acknowledge as one of their very best of the era, "Far beyond the realms of pop, jazz or anything," to quote the man himself.

Live performances: *Never performed live.*

HOTS ON FOR NOWHERE
PAGE, PLANT
STUDIO: MUSICLAND

Light and airy and vaguely swingish, 'Hots On For Nowhere' delights in its off-the-wall quirkiness. Its basic structure can be traced to the rehearsal sessions for the sixth album as well as the '75 era live versions of 'Dazed And Confused'. Plant unfolds more tales from Malibu, taking a swing at his close friends in the process and throwing in plenty of 'oohs' and 'ahs' for good measure. He later revealed that the accusations levelled at 'friends who would give me fuck all' were aimed at Page and Peter Grant who for some reason had incurred his displeasure.

Page meanwhile makes full use of the tremolo arm on the new blue Strat, as he pulls out a ridiculous twang in the middle of a delightful solo. From the moment Plant shouts, 'Oh, I lost my way home!' Bonzo roars in with some decorative fills, and Page takes it all out on a blistering babble of notes. Friendly.

This track's odd time signature was echoed some 18 years later in the impressive Page/David Coverdale collaboration 'Pride And Joy'.

Live performances: *Never performed live.*

TEA FOR ONE
PAGE, PLANT
STUDIO: MUSICLAND

A relaxed blues winds up the proceedings. Lyrically Robert reflects on the post accident period when he was separated from his wife Maureen. 'Tea For One' definitely tries to recapture the spirit of their earlier, self-penned blues epic 'Since I've Been Loving You'. Unfortunately it never matches that number for excitement. The solo is adequately applied in the expected tradition, but cannot hide the fact that the song itself is a trifle dull. A low key exit.

Live performances: *Never performed live.*

NB: *The lack of live interpretations of the 'Presence' material is quite striking; however, given that it was to be a full year before they returned to the road, perhaps understandable. Had they been able to tour off the back of its release, we may well have enjoyed live takes of 'Candy Store Rock' etc.*

LED·ZEPPELIN

THE SOUNDTRACK FROM THE FILM
THE SONG REMAINS THE SAME

SOUNDTRACK FROM THE FiLM THE SONG REMAiNS THE SAME

SWAN SONG

89402

Within six months there was another Zeppelin album in the shops, the soundtrack album to their much maligned feature film.

There had been previous attempts to produce a Led Zeppelin movie before The Song Remains The Same. Back in 1970, footage from gigs at the Albert Hall, the spring US tour and a trip to Iceland in June were professionally filmed at the request of manager Peter Grant with a view to assembling an hour-long special for TV distribution. Filming in Japan the next year also took place, but the project never materialised.

The story then shifts to May 1973. Film maker Joe Massot approached Jimmy and Peter during the group's mid-tour break with a view to shooting their return leg. The offer was turned down by Grant who told Massot they had plans to make their own film with a famous director.

However, at the tail end of the two-legged, hugely successful American trip, they changed their minds. A call went out from Grant to Joe Massot on July 14. Massot and crew flew over and filmed various backstage shots, screen tested the stage act at gigs in Baltimore and Pittsburgh and then filmed all three of their Madison Square Garden dates on July 27, 28 and 29. These shows were recorded by Eddie Kramer and formed the basis of the resulting soundtrack album. (All the tracks were later mixed down at Electric Lady in New York and Trident Studios in London.)

Coming at the end of a gruelling tour, these particular performances were hardly magic nights. However, as this was the music that matched the footage, it had to be made available.

There had been plans to shoot some more

film on the aborted world tour of 1975/76. After Robert's accident, though, with short term plans for live gigs an impossibility, Page used this period of inactivity to tie up the movie and soundtrack, using the footage shot with Joe Massot and employing Peter Clifton to arrange the technical aspects. The movie poster and sleeve design depicted a run down picture house, which was based on Old Street studios, a London rehearsal theatre they used to perfect the 1973 US stage act prior to touring.

The film was premièred in New York on October 21, with the album hitting the stores the next day. It reached number one in the UK but had to settle for second place in the States. The film went on to become a staple diet of late night movie houses for years to come, and its subsequent issue on video in 1984 has provided a whole new generation of fans with a front row seat on Led Zeppelin.

It has to be said, though, that it's only an adequate representation. Visually and musically their live shows after 1973 were much more spectacular. It's a great shame that there is no official visual record of Earls Court 1975, the US 1977 tour or Knebworth. All these shows were filmed for the group and

remain in the archives. Having been privileged enough to have seen these video tapes, I can endorse the fact that they capture the magic of the live Led Zeppelin far better than the official *The Song Remains The Same* movie.

Much the same can be said of the soundtrack album. Keen collectors will know of far better material that has surfaced unofficially. In retrospect, performances such as 'Moby Dick' and 'Dazed And Confused' sound somewhat lack-lustre, and the whole question of the actual track listing still baffles. Why, for instance, does 'Celebration Day' appear on the soundtrack album but is nowhere to be seen (or heard) in the film? How come sizzling filmed performances of 'Since I've Been Loving You' and 'Heartbreaker' were somehow left off the album? These anomalies all point to the fact that, as Page admitted at the time, *The Song Remains The Same* movie and soundtrack proved to be a rare Led Zeppelin compromise.

Studios: all live material recorded at Madison Square Garden, New York, July 27, 28 and 29, 1973. Mixed at Electric Lady, New York, and Trident, London.

Above: Earls Court, London, 1975;
below, on stage, 1975.

*The front man, Robert Plant, 1971 (above)
and 1972 (inset).*

The engine room – John Bonham.

The world's greatest live attraction...
...slaying America, 1977.

The keyboard wizard, John Paul Jones, in the mid-seventies, and, above, as bassman.

*The alchemist,
Jimmy Page,
with the Gibson
double-neck,
1977, and
with Gibson
Les Paul, 1975.*

Top: the acoustic set, 1977; and below, the Live Aid reunion, July 13, 1985.

ROCK AND ROLL
BONHAM, JONES, PAGE, PLANT

A fine opening gambit. For the live version Plant sings in a lower key and Page duck walks into the solo. Vibrant.

CELEBRATION DAY
JONES, PAGE, PLANT

In the movie, 'Rock And Roll' is edited into 'Black Dog'. The album, however, has the authentic link into 'Celebration Day'. Strangely edited out of the film, this underrated stage number sounds spot on. Jimmy is particularly impressive weaving a cluster of notes towards the outro. Revives memories of its Knebworth airing.

THE SONG REMAINS THE SAME
PAGE, PLANT

An excellent live take with Page switching to the double-neck. In the film, it accompanies Plant's Arthurian fantasy sequence, snippets of which he would later use as a backdrop to 'Immigrant Song' on his 1990 solo tour.

THE RAIN SONG
PAGE, PLANT

Dovetails from 'The Song Remains The Same' as was the custom during this era. This version includes some delicate Page strumming and precise Bonham dynamics. At times, though, the mellotron quivers a little unsteadily.

DAZED AND CONFUSED
PAGE

Stripped of the on-stage visuals, this marathon loses its appeal somewhat. There are some high spots, the San Francisco sequence, the bow interlude with its stereo panning and the guitar-vocal interplay. Elsewhere it becomes excessive and lumbering.

NO QUARTER
JONES, PAGE, PLANT

The album's standout performance. Everything works perfectly here, from Jones' revolving opening through to a simply divine Page solo. A slightly different version appears in the film.

STAIRWAY TO HEAVEN
PAGE, PLANT

'Stairway' had yet to take on truly epic proportions during this era, and it followed 'Dazed And Confused' in the set. Such was the excitement of that number, the audience often drowned out the intro to 'Stairway'. Madison Square Garden was one such venue. Though the album version gives little away, the live outtakes reveal Plant trying to settle the audience down. The intro link retained for the album has Plant saying, "This is a song of hope." It edits out his next line: "And it's a very quiet song… so shurrup!"

MOBY DICK
BONHAM, JONES, PLANT

Another track that loses most of its impact without the visual footage. In the movie it makes a perfect accompaniment to Bonzo's profile. On record it goes on much too long. A far better idea here would have been to insert the 'Heartbreaker' segment that precedes 'Whole Lotta Love' in the film, run through to the 'Whole Lotta Love' track and then add 'The Ocean' as an encore. Both these tracks were left on the splicing block.

WHOLE LOTTA LOVE
BONHAM, JONES, PAGE, PLANT

In the film, as in all the shows on the tour, 'Whole Lotta Love' segued in from 'Heartbreaker'. Here it's edited to appear as a track in its own right. Complete with Jimmy on vocals, 'The Crunge' sequence, the theramin attack, and 'Let That Boy Boogie', it sustains the interest. A live version of the revamped arrangement they played at Knebworth would be most welcome.

The following tracks appear in the film but not on the record: 'Black Dog', 'Since I've Been Loving You' and 'Heartbreaker'. Jimmy's solo piece from 'Physical Graffiti', 'Bron-Y-Aur', is also heard in the film. Another number, copyrighted as 'Autumn Lake', is played on a hurdy gurdy by Page in an early pre-concert sequence. Other songs known to have been aired at the Madison Square Garden gigs and likely to have been recorded and filmed are: 'Over The Hills And Far Away', 'Misty Mountain Hop', 'The Ocean', 'Communication Breakdown' and 'Thank You'. 'The Ocean' has surfaced on an outtake film track unofficial tape that also has the 'Heartbreaker'/'Whole Lotta Love' sequence and alternate takes of 'Stairway To Heaven' and 'Moby Dick'.

iN THROUGH THE OUT DOOR

SWAN SONG

59410

After a two-year absence, dictated by the tragic death of Robert Plant's young son Karac from a stomach infection, Led Zeppelin finally became active again. This album was recorded at the tail end of 1978 at Abba's Polar Music studio in Stockholm.

Unlike the urgency of Munich in 1975, the Swedish expedition was a much more relaxed affair. Most of the new songs had been well rehearsed in London and there was no need for the studio composing method of earlier recording sessions. They knew what they had to do, and made full use of the studio facilities with Leif Masses and Lennart Ostlund on hand to engineer it all.

The most significant musical contribution came from John Paul Jones. With tongue planted firmly in cheek, he said at the time that his considerable influence on proceedings was due to his arrival at the studio earlier than his colleagues on most days. With lead composing credits on all but one of the seven tracks selected for the album, his contribution was immense.

Rollicking piano on 'South Bound Suarez', an Argentine soccer chant burst midway through 'Fool In The Rain', a *Gone With The Wind* string-synth intro for 'I'm Gonna Crawl'

and a cluster of classically sounding notes on 'All My Love' - all this was the work of the group's lowest profile member.

The mixing was wrapped up with further sessions in early 1979. There had been talk of a European tour slated for around February. Ultimately they decided to dispense with any conventional gigging (perhaps erroneously), and return to the concert platform in the grandest possible fashion: two shows in August 1979 at the open air Knebworth Park, estimated capacity 300,000 plus.

The completed album, rumoured in some

circles to be titled 'Look', was held back from release to coincide with the Knebworth shows. In a rare lapse of marketing strategy, the album missed the concert deadline, appearing a week after Knebworth on August 20. Not that it made a scrap of difference. The record, eventually titled 'In Through The Out Door' because, as Jimmy put it, "That's the hardest way to get back in", was rapturously received around the world. It made number one in the UK in its first week and number one in America in its second. It also instantly topped the charts in Japan, New Zealand, Australia and Germany. In the first 10 days of release its sales topped two million.

It was in America though, that the real sales phenomena occurred. Its release was heralded as a saviour to the then flagging US record industry. It generated massive store traffic as it held the top spot for seven weeks. Even more remarkable was the renewed demand for previous Zepp albums. Atlantic shifted a staggering one million back catalogue albums during September 1979, a situation that resulted in Led Zeppelin's entire catalogue appearing on the *Billboard* Top 200 during the weeks of October 27 and November 3. This beat the previous record for most albums on the chart set in 1975 held by… you guessed it, Led Zeppelin.

What made these figures all the more staggering was that during Led Zeppelin's absence from the music scene during the previous two years punk rock had emerged, and a central philosophy of punk was its contrary stance to – and general loathing of – massively popular 'stadium' bands like Led Zeppelin who, it was claimed, were now redundant in the new era. These claims were taken up by newly appointed, young and somewhat hawkish staff at the various UK music magazines, all of which claimed to be arbiters of taste in rock. Such claims might have been fashionable but they were as preposterous as they were premature: it was Led Zeppelin – not the punks – who sold the most records in the new era, just as they had in the old. (It was also Led Zeppelin who won the annual readers' polls in these magazines, much to the chagrin of the editorial staff who championed punk!)

Then there was the album's sleeve. Easily their most ambitious to date, the brief to Hipgnosis was simple enough. They all felt the album to be fresh, new and direct. The album sleeve was to indicate just that. Designer Aubrey Powell felt some of the music had a barrel-house, bayou bar, late night blues feel to it. On Page's suggestion, he worked on a bar room scene, travelling to New Orleans to gain some reference. (Some reports indicate the bar as being the Old Absinthe Bar at 400 Bourbon Street, just around the corner from the Royal Orleans hotel.)

On his return, the Hipgnosis team built a New Orleans bar room scene at Shepperton studios, shooting six different scenes. These sepia toned photos formed the six alternate sleeves that were issued, each one depicting the view from the six characters in the scene. To indicate that freshness, or a new lick of paint as Powell described it, an area was wiped clean on each print. This outer stroke led Jimmy to request that the inner bag be prepared in such a way that it would colour when water was applied.

Finally Peter Grant insisted all the sleeves be shrink wrapped into a brown paper bag so that no buyer would know which sleeve he would be receiving, and also to prove that you could stuff a Led Zepp album into a paper bag and it would still sell! And of course it did.

Musically, 'In Through The Out Door' is dominated by John Paul Jones. His influence is stronger than ever before. Disappointingly, the album suffers from a less than crystal clear production, and in hindsight, did possess more than its quota of filler material. Still, what's good is very good indeed, and at the time was indication enough to suggest that Led Zeppelin were ready to enter the new decade with as much enthusiasm as they had entered the Seventies.

IN THE EVENING
JONES, PAGE, PLANT
STUDIOS: POLAR MUSIC, STOCKHOLM;
PLUMPTON, SUSSEX

To illustrate the feeling of rebirth, Page pulls out the old violin bow to create a dramatic opening segment (reminiscent of his work on the soundtrack of Kenneth Anger's *Lucifer Rising*). From there on, this is a very satisfying flexing of the muscles.

Jimmy also used a Gizmatron (an effect invented by Lol Creme and Kevin Godley of 10cc) device to increase distortion and create the slamming door effect heard at the onset of

the solo. Plant's arrogant strutting vocal is undercut by a majestic cascading riff that ricochets off every wall. When the whole thing slows up momentarily, some shimmering minor chords and fluid bass take control. Then it's headlong into a powerful fade. A performance that pushed its chest out as if to say... take that. Clearly Led Zeppelin still had... it.

Live performances: *Premièred at the Copenhagen shows, and in for Knebworth where it stood out as a stunning new creation, entering the set for Page's visual violin bow segment. Also used on the 'Over Europe' 1980 tour. Page played the string-bending blue Strat on this track. Plant then revived the number to great effect on his 'Now And Zen' solo tour in 1988.*

SOUTH BOUND SUAREZ
JONES, PLANT
STUDIOS: POLAR MUSIC; PLUMPTON

With its rollicking piano intro, this is a track that conjures up the Louisiana/New Orleans bar room feel of the sleeve. Plant's vocals are somewhat strained and overall the only redeeming feature of a rather lack-lustre outing is a measured Page solo and the do-wop fade out.

Live performances: *Never performed live.*

FOOL IN THE RAIN
JONES, PAGE, PLANT
STUDIO: POLAR MUSIC

During the summer of 1978, the World Cup was played out in Argentina against a variety of samba-inspired TV soccer themes. Those South American themes were still ringing in the ears of Plant and Jones when Led Zeppelin reconvened to plan this album. Thus the idea emerged to layer on their own samba half way through the hop-skip riff arrangement of this tune. Crazy as it sounds, it works beautifully right through J.P.'s street whistles to Bonzo's delightfully constructed timpani crashes. Back at mid tempo, Jimmy puts in a quite exquisite solo. A most successful alliance that grew out of Plant's insistence that new territory had to be investigated if they were to sustain his own personal commitment, a point thrashed out at their rehearsal sessions at Clearwell Castle in May of 1978. 'Fool In The Rain' became their sixth US Top 40 hit when it reached number 21 in January 1980.

Live performances: *Never performed live.*

HOT DOG
PAGE, PLANT
STUDIO: POLAR MUSIC; PLUMPTON

'Hot Dog' owes much to the state of Texas and to the state of a particular female in Texas. Musically it grew out of their London pre-production rehearsals, where as usual they began by running through old Elvis Presley and Ricky Nelson material from the Fifties. A rockabilly country hoe-down, it was obviously great fun to record and did develop into a crowd pleaser on the European tour (though it sounded a

little mystifying on its Knebworth première).
On record though, time has not been too kind
to it, and as for that solo... are you putting us
on J. Page?

Live performances: *Brought in for
Copenhagen and Knebworth and retained for
all the 1980 'Over Europe' dates. An official
promo video of this track, filmed at
Knebworth, was made available by Swan
Song to the record industry in America.*

CAROUSELAMBRA
JONES, PAGE, PLANT
STUDIO: POLAR MUSIC; PLUMPTON

The epic. Driven along relentlessly by Jones'
keyboard thrusts, 'Carouselambra' is a typically grandiose Zeppelin marathon. It was first
conceived in rehearsal at their Clearwell
Castle get-together in May 1978. This is one
of the only tracks cut in the studio that
employs the Gibson double-neck guitar, which
can be heard to great effect played by Page
during the slower middle section.

Lyrically, this is a typically mystical affair
made even more obscure by a very muddy mix

that all but buries Plant's vocal. Allegedly, it
harks back to the past to act as a shroud for a
contemporary Plant observation of a person
who in his words will one day realise it was
written about them and proclaim... "My God!
Was it really like that?"

'Carouselambra' covers a lot of ground
during its 10-minute duration, and though
the actual recording restricts its majestic
quality somewhat, the intentions here
remain honourable.

Live performances: *Sadly, never played live.
They had planned to work on an arrangement
of this for 'Led Zeppelin: The 1980's
Campaign'. It certainly had the scope to be a
compelling live piece.*

ALL MY LOVE
JONES, PLANT
STUDIOS: POLAR MUSIC; PLUMPTON

As can be observed from the composing credits, this came from an occasion when Plant
and Jones arrived at the studio first. A very
successful attempt to write a melodic, pretty
love song, the lyrics are full of sincerity, inspir-

ing Robert to turn in a superb vocal performance. Jones' classical keyboard solo is another revelation, while Jimmy adds some subtle acoustic picking. 'All My Love' mirrors the reflective and mellow mood Plant found himself in during 1978. That he could still transfer those feelings into the group's music proved to them that collectively Led Zeppelin remained very much in the present tense.

N.B. There exists a wonderful, extended alternative version of 'All My Love'. It clocks in at seven minutes and two seconds and has a complete ending, with Plant echoing his 'I get a bit lonely' sentiments in an arrangement that was later employed on the 1980 live version. The original two inch master reel of this outtake as recorded at Polar Studios on November 14, 1978, is labelled 'The Hook', a working title which probably refers to the commercial nature of the song.

Live performances: *The only previously untried number inserted into the 'Over Europe' tour in 1980. It became one of the best received performances of the whole tour.*

I'M GONNA CRAWL
JONES, PAGE, PLANT
STUDIOS: POLAR MUSIC; PLUMPTON

Enhanced by yet another major Jones contribution, this time a smooth synthesised string arrangement, 'I'm Gonna Crawl' is a relaxed and confident slow blues. Plant saw this as an attempt to capture the laid-back approach of the mid-Sixties work of Wilson Pickett, O.V. Wright and Otis Redding, Pickett's 'It's Too Late' being a particular reference point. Some forceful Bonham sparring with Page brings a typical dynamic quality to the proceedings, while Jimmy's solo is his best slow blues performance since the third album. A pleading Plant vocal brings the track to a satisfying finale.

Live performances: *Never performed live.*

CODA

LED·ZEPPELIN

CODA

SWAN SONG

A0051

During 1981 there was much speculation within the inner Swan Song sanctum over whether a final album would be delivered. The original Swan Song contract signed with Atlantic in 1974, called for five albums. With no intention of keeping the group together in any form, contractual and business reasons therefore led Page, Plant and Jones to go ahead with a final album project.

The intention was to profile their 12-year career with a collection of quality left-over tracks. Page began shifting through the tapes at his Sol recording studio in Berkshire during the summer of 1981. After completing the *Death Wish II* soundtrack, he called in Robert and J. P. to mix, and in some cases overdub, the eight selected tracks. The album had a working title of 'Early Days And Latter Days' and was compiled for release early in 1982. Its eventual release was held over until Robert's début solo set 'Pictures At Eleven' hit the shops in the summer.

The sleeve involved collating a selection of off-stage group photos to form a centre spread collage. Ideas thrown around at a meeting the author had with Page and Plant in March 1982 to discuss this projected sleeve, ranged from using stills from their Knebworth rehearsal video filmed at Bray studios in June 1979, to digging up some celebrated 'road fever' pics from the 1973 US tour.·Both of those ideas (in the latter case not surprisingly!) were ultimately vetoed. The final 30 photographs were eventually housed in a grey outer sleeve simply engraved with the words Led Zeppelin and 'Coda', an appropriate revised title, defined in the dictionary as, "An independent passage introduced after the main part of a movement."

'Coda' was released on November 22, 1982, with little pre-publicity. A low-key advertising campaign employing posters with a symbolic illustration of nine mysterious discs, backed it up. In the UK, only the traditional crop of seasonal TV-advertised titles prevented it reaching the top spot. It entered and stayed at number four. In America 'Coda' reached a credible sixth on the *Billboard* chart.

The release of 'Coda' neatly tied up the loose recorded ends and it remains an enjoyable and affectionate summary of the Led Zeppelin era – chronicling their studio development during the years 1969 to 1978 – with plenty of previously unheard surprises along the way.

WE'RE GONNA GROOVE
B.B. KING,
STUDIOS: BETHEA STUDIO: MORGAN, LONDON; THE SOL, BERKSHIRE

One of the great 'lost' Zepp performances finally receives an official airing. 'We're Gonna Groove' was recorded during a hectic week in June 1969 when their schedule ran as follows:
Saturday: gig at Bristol Colston Hall.
Tuesday: radio session for John Peel's *Top Gear* in Bond Street, London.
Wednesday: recording session at Morgan studios London.
Thursday: gig at Portsmouth Guild Hall.
Friday: radio concert for the BBC at the Playhouse Theatre London.
Saturday: live appearance at the Bath Festival Of Blues.
Sunday: 6pm and 9pm appearances at the

Royal Albert Hall Pop Proms, London.

Phew! No time for a two-year lay off in those days. 'We're Gonna Groove' was chosen as their set opener on the UK, Europe and US dates in early 1970, and will have already been familiar to keen Zepp collectors as a live bootleg track. This studio version, somehow deemed unusable for 'Led Zeppelin II', is full of slashing Page guitar (with sub-octivider effects added at The Sol in 1982), great Bonham percussion and typically frantic Plant vocal.

Live performances: *The set opener of the UK, European and US dates January to April 1970, it was then discarded in favour of 'Immigrant Song'.*

POOR TOM
PAGE, PLANT
STUDIOS: OLYMPIC, LONDON; THE SOL

One of the 'Zeppelin III' leftovers from the June 1970 sessions at Olympic, 'Poor Tom' is another product of the trip to Bron-Y-Aur. A semi-acoustic bluesy jugband work-out, it's propelled along by an inventive Bonham shuf-fle that holds up the momentum all the way through. Plant throws in some harmonica blowing for good measure.

Live performances: *Never performed live.*

I CAN'T QUIT YOU BABY
WILLIE DIXON
STUDIO: LIVE SOUND CHECK RECORDING FROM
THE ROYAL ALBERT HALL, MIXED AT THE SOL

Monday, January 9, 1970, is the next dateline revisited. This alleged soundcheck rehearsal run-through of a first album blues standard does, in fact, sound very similar to the actual live version performed in the evening (as captured on film by the crew employed to work on the intended Led Zeppelin documentary). Did the tapes get mislabelled? Well whatever version it is, this a great example of Led Zeppelin, the blues band, having a blow and enjoying every minute of it.

Live performances: *Included in the set from 1968 through to the fifth US tour in 1970. Revived as part of the 'Whole Lotta Love' medley for the Japan, UK and Europe dates*

CODA : THE TEN ALBUM LEGACY

1972/3. Also rehearsed at the Atlantic reunion in May 1988.

WALTER'S WALK
PAGE, PLANT
STUDIOS: STARGROVES, BERKSHIRE, WITH THE
ROLLING STONES' MOBILE; THE SOL

An unexpected gem. Laid down in May 1972 with Eddie Kramer and left off 'Houses Of The Holy', 'Walter's Walk' is a tense, unmelodic rocker spearheaded by a solid Page riff. The overall sound here shares little of the crispness of most of the 'Houses' material. Only the drumming brings to mind that particular era. It obviously didn't fit into the game plan of the time, but emerges as a dense and intoxicating outing.

It's quite possible that this song existed only as a basic backing track until the band put 'Coda' together. Plant's vocal delivery sounds very Eighties in feel (not unlike 'Burning Down One Side' from his first solo album) and it could well be that a new vocal was recorded at The Sol Studios in early 1982.

Live performances: *Never performed live in its*

entirety, the basic structure of 'Walter's Walk' was, however, employed during 'Dazed And Confused' at least once on the 1972 US tour.

OZONE BABY
PAGE, PLANT
STUDIOS: POLAR MUSIC, STOCKHOLM; THE SOL

It's back to November 1978 for an 'Out Door' left-over. 'Ozone Baby' has an affable exuberance spurred on by Plant, who smiles through the whole thing. Up-tempo and friendly, its charm is further enhanced by a fluttering Page solo and some harmonised vocal effects.

Live performances: *Never performed live.*

DARLENE
BONHAM, JONES, PAGE, PLANT
STUDIOS: POLAR MUSIC; THE SOL

Two days later in Stockholm we join the boys for a jiving rock'n'roll jam. 'Darlene' is just that. Starting out as a jerkily riffed, playful exercise with tinkling Jones piano and off beat drumming, it develops into a rousing fade out with Page pulling out some classic James Burton licks.

Live performances: *Never performed live.*

BONZO'S MONTREUX
BONHAM
STUDIOS: MOUNTAIN, MONTREUX; THE SOL

The oft-touted, total percussion number Bonzo cut with Jimmy during their exile in Montreux in September 1976. Bonham includes all manner of percussive effects here, aided by Jimmy's electronic treatments. A tuneful pattern does emerge from the soloing, primarily a high pitched steel drum sound created by Page's newly acquired harmoniser. An affectionate if unspectacular tribute, though hardly the best showcase for John Bonham's vast talent.

Live performances: Never performed live.

WEARING AND TEARING
PAGE, PLANT
STUDIOS: POLAR MUSIC; THE SOL

A final Tuesday rendezvous with Led Zeppelin in the Abba studios. Recorded on November 21, 1978, 'Wearing And Tearing' is the number Page and Plant had threatened would keep up with the punk rock bands in London. It was also the track nearly made available to the 300,000-plus Knebworth audience.

Thankfully it sees the light of day here. This vibrant Plant plea for the right cure takes off at breakneck speed, side-stepping periodically to let Plant *a cappella* the lines *à la* 'Black Dog'. It gets more and more frantic with Page playing at a frightening pace, supported by that ever steady Bonham/Jones rhythm section. The intensity accelerates until the song hots up to an abrupt ending.

Live performances: *Never performed live in the Zeppelin era, though it was slated to emerge in the 'Led Zeppelin: The Eighties Campaign'. Twelve years on it was a live vehicle with which Plant and Page would wow the Knebworth 1990 audience. The 1990 live delivery of the final track on the tenth Led Zeppelin album proved yet again the sheer potency of their material when in the hands of the original composers. For a few short minutes the song really did remain the same...*

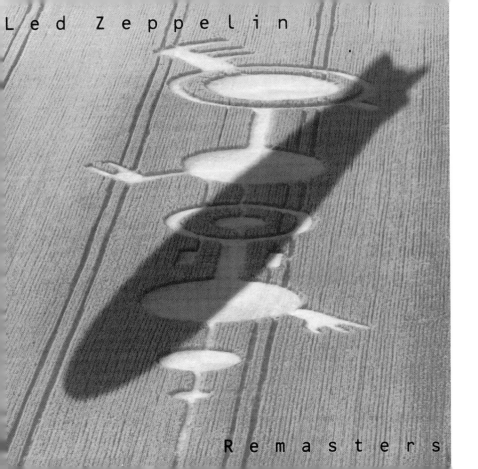

LED ZEPPELIN REMASTERED 1990 & 1993

SWAN SONG
89402

LED ZEPPELIN

ATLANTIC 7567821441/2/4 (SIX ALBUMS, FOUR CDS, FOUR CASSETTES)

Whole Lotta Love / Heartbreaker / Communication Breakdown / Babe I'm Gonna Leave You / What Is And What Should Never Be / Thank You / I Can't Quit You Baby / Dazed And Confused / Your Time Is Gonna Come / Ramble On / Travelling Riverside Blues / Friends / Celebration Day / Hey Hey What Can I Do / White Summer, Black Mountain Side / Black Dog / Over The Hills And Far Away / Immigrant Song / The Battle Of Evermore / Bron-Y-Aur Stomp / Tangerine / Going To California / Since I've Been Loving You/D'Yer Mak'er / Gallows Pole / Custard Pie / Misty Mountain Hop / Rock And Roll / The Rain Song / Stairway To Heaven / Kashmir / Trampled Underfoot / For Your Life / No Quarter / Dancing Days / When The Levee Breaks / Achilles Last Stand / The Song Remains The Same / Ten Years Gone / In My Time Of Dying / In The Evening / Candy Store Rock / The Ocean / Ozone Baby / Houses Of the Holy /Wearing And Tearing/Poor Tom / Nobody's Fault But Mine / Fool In The Rain / In The Light / The Wanton Song / Moby Dick-Bonzo's Montreux / I'm Gonna Crawl / All My Love

REMASTERS

ATLANTIC ZEP 1/7567804152/4 (TRIPLE ALBUM, DOUBLE CD, DOUBLE CASSETTE)

Communication Breakdown / Babe I'm Gonna Leave You / Good Times, Bad Times / Dazed And Confused / Heartbreaker / Whole Lotta Love / Ramble On / Since I've Been Loving

You / Celebration Day / Immigrant Song / Black Dog, Rock And Roll / Battle Of Evermore / Stairway To Heaven / The Song Remains The Same / D'yer Mak'er / No Quarter / Houses Of The Holy / Trampled Underfoot / Kashmir / Nobody's Fault But Mine / Achilles Last Stand / All My Love / In The Evening (Cassette and CD versions also include Misty Mountain Hop / The Rain Song)

The release of these two separate Led Zeppelin retrospective collections in the space of two weeks in October 1990, rounded off a year in which the group's popularity reached heights unparalleled since the mid-Seventies. The excitement that greeted the appearance of the 'Led Zeppelin Remastered' project emphasised how much the group – and the timeless and eclectic quality of their music – had been missed during the 'disposable pop' atmosphere of the Eighties.

The whole exercise was a tremendous success, both critically and commercially. Reviewers who had previously been cold towards Led Zeppelin felt obliged to reconsider their opinions in the light of their influence and the obvious fact that so many of those groups that followed in their wake were noticeably inferior in every department. And for a boxed set costing almost £50 sales throughout the world were extraordinary. Much of this may have been due to the fact that Led Zeppelin's catalogue had never been tastelessly exploited in the same way that, say, The Who or The Stones' had been. That there had never been a Led Zep 'Best Of' compilation before – and the aftermath of its eventual release – was surely a further indication of the astuteness of Peter Grant's long term management strategies.

It had been no secret that Jimmy Page was deeply unhappy with the Led Zeppelin CDs that Atlantic issued without consulting him. Originally produced for vinyl, the music suffered in transit: subtle frequencies in the sound spectrum were lost and the 'ambient' sound that Page had worked so hard to create by the sensitive placement of microphones in the studio was also lost. Small wonder, then, that when Atlantic approached him to remaster the tapes for a compilation collection, he jumped at the idea. Studio time was booked at New York's Sterling studios where Page spent a week in May 1990 with engineer

George Marino digitally restoring the bulk of Led Zeppelin's catalogue from the original two-track master tapes.

The plan was to compile a multi-track box set collection for which Page drew up a possible listing for Plant and Jones to sanction. "I really wanted to improve the overall sound spectrum," Page was quoted on the official press release. "Basically it's the same picture with a different frame."

John Paul Jones added: "The songs sound as fresh today as they did when first recorded, and the new positions in the running order seem to put them in a totally different light."

The original compilation concept was to package 54 tracks in a de-luxe box with accompanying booklet of photos and essays. Atlantic's European distributors, East West, also managed to clear a separate edited version of the set for Europe only. This condensed version, virtually a greatest hits package aimed squarely at the lucrative Christmas market, appeared under the title 'Remasters' as a 24-track, triple album and 26-track, double CD and cassette on October 15. A full marketing campaign including a TV advertisement was prepared as the Zepp catalogue

finally succumbed to the Nineties commercial treatment. Plant, Page and Jones did retain part of their original strategy in vetoing the planned release of 'Stairway To Heaven' as a UK single.

The 'Remasters' set was deleted in the UK

in the summer of 1991, and since it contains one track not on the box set ('Good Times Bad Times'), it is sure to be a future Zepp vinyl collectable. After a period of withdrawal the set reappeared on catalogue in 1992 on CD and cassette. It was also eventually issued in America as a three CD set with a bonus 'Led Zeppelin Profiled' official interview promo CD. The real gem for Zeppelin enthusiasts was the October 29 appearance of the 54 track box set, simply entitled 'Led Zeppelin' and spread over six albums, four CD's and four cassettes.

Despite certain faults - the dearth of selections from 'Physical Graffiti', no chronological live tracks or alternate studio takes, the factual errors in the visually superb accompanying booklet (Live Aid in 1987!) - this set does stand as a lasting testament to the diverse musical styles Led Zeppelin approached from 1968 to 1980. Beautifully packaged with a typically enigmatic design featuring the shadow of an airship over those myserious cornfield circles (which perhaps suggested that Led Zeppelin were somehow responsible for – or at least knew *something* about – their appearance in the first place), it's wonderful to hear so many tracks all at one sitting. For those

very familiar with their catalogue, the new sequencing is also a joy – as 'Heartbreaker' switches instantly to 'Communication Breakdown', 'Over The Hills And Far Away' juxtaposes against 'Immigrant Song' and 'The Song Remains The Same' drifts into 'Ten Years Gone'. Note too, the slightly longer intro to 'Nobody's Fault But Mine' with an extra opening Page guitar riff, and the fact that many timings on the original albums were well out (e.g. 'Kashmir' is now correctly listed as being 8.31 in duration, and not the long presumed 9.41).

And there are some new delights. The little heard 'Zeppelin III' era 'Hey Hey What Can I Do', previously available only on a long-deleted UK Atlantic sampler album, and as the B-side to the 1970 'Immigrant Song' US/European single, retains all its original summer of 1970 semi-acoustic warmth. It's also great to hear the spiralling blues slide of the BBC *Top Gear* 1969 radio remnant 'Travelling Riverside Blues' – a Page/Plant/ Robert Johnson interpretation. Nostalgic memories also prevail on the live BBC take of 'White Summer/Black Mountain Side' from June 27, 1969. Jimmy has also included an

affectionate Bonzo tribute, an amalgamation of 'Moby Dick' and 'Bonzo's Montreux', produced with the aid of Synclavier programming at Atlantic's Synclavier suite.

All in all, the overall sound quality is greatly enhanced, with Page adding a new punch and clarity remastered from the original analogue tapes.

The reception the boxed set received exceeded even Atlantic's own high expectations. By the end of 1992 it had shifted over a million units worldwide, making it the best selling historical retrospective package of its kind, an extraordinary testament to Led Zeppelin's ongoing power, influence and popularity.

The previously unreleased material is analysed below.

TRAVELLING RIVERSIDE BLUES

PAGE, PLANT, ROBERT JOHNSON

RECORDED AT MAIDA VALE STUDIO, LONDON

One of the legendary Zepp BBC performances recorded on June 24, 1969, by John Waters at the BBC's Maida Vale Studio. This was one of the few BBC tracks on which Page was able to dub extra guitar tracks. An adaptation of an old Robert Johnson tune, it was initially aired on John Peel's *Top Gear* show on Sunday June 28, 1969, under the title 'Travelling Riverside Blues '69'. Its renown in collecting circles is largely due to the fact that it was a special recording intended only for radio broadcast. It was interest from US radio interviewers and fans during his 'Outrider' tour that led him to negotiate with BBC Enterprises for its release on the boxed set. A video promo with outtake footage from *The Song Remains The Same* was cut together for use by MTV and other interested TV outlets.

The track itself is a superb remnant from mid-'69, and remains for me one of their most complete performances, not least for Page's wonderful slide guitar work and Plant's teasing ad libs ("Ahh why doncha come in my kitchen"). A superbly packaged one track promo CD single was issued for radio play in the US, which resulted in the track reaching number seven on the *Billboard* Top Rock Tracks Top 50 chart in November 1990, culled from national album rock radio airplay reports. In my extensive collection, this promo CD takes pride of place as my favourite CD single of all time.

WHITE SUMMER/BLACK MOUNTAIN SIDE
PAGE
RECORDED LIVE AT THE LONDON PLAYHOUSE
THEATRE FOR BBC RADIO

This recording comes from the live broadcast made from the Playhouse Theatre on June 27, 1969, for the pilot programme of Radio One's *In Concert* series. Zeppelin's involvement came about after Jimmy told producer Jeff Griffin that Zeppelin had enjoyed recording for *Top Gear* but felt the scope of the session didn't allow them sufficient time to display what the band could achieve. Griffin told Jimmy he was trying to get a one hour concert special off the ground and invited Zepp to record the pilot programme. Broadcast on August 10, 1969, it set the seal on the long running *In Concert* series which began a regular spot the following January.

The '69 In Concert has been much boot-legged and many fans will already be familiar with the 'White Summer'/'Black Mountain Side' segment. It was a staple inclusion of the mid-'69 to early '70 dates, and gives Page an opportunity to indulge in a bit of the old CIA, accompanied on timpani and other assorted percussion by John Bonham.

HEY HEY WHAT CAN I DO
PAGE, PLANT, JONES, BONHAM
STUDIO: ISLAND, LONDON

This track has long been a much sought after Zepp rarity and its inclusion on the box is most welcome. A product of the easygoing summer of 1970 sessions at Island Studios, having been conceived in rehearsal at Bron-Y-Aur and Headley Grange, it is one of the most relaxed and commercial group compositions of this era, managing to balance the new found mellowness with the familiar dynamics. Note for example how Robert places just the right emphasis on the line "Gotta little woman and she won't be true", and just when you expect a switch to the cranked up Marshall amps they allow the song to slip back into a warm country flavoured mandolin led melody. The collapsing finale recalls the finish of 'In My Time Of Dying'.

All in all, this deserved a wider platform instead of being tucked away on the B-side to the US single of 'Immigrant Song' and as a token attraction on the obscure 'New Age Of Atlantic' sampler.

MOBY DICK/BONZO'S MONTREUX
PAGE, JONES, BONHAM

STUDIOS: MIRROR SOUND, LOS ANGELES, MAYFAIR,
NEW YORK, A&R, NEW YORK (MOBY DICK);
MOUNTAIN, MONTREUX, THE SOL, COOKHAM
(BONZO'S MONTREUX)

Although strictly speaking this is not really new or unheard material, the amalgamation is. It came about after Jimmy scanned the lists the others had compiled and found both these titles prominently featured. The idea to combine elements of both tracks came after he'd checked the tempo on a metronome. During the remastering period, Jimmy booked into the Atlantic Synclavier Suite in New York and, with help from John Mahoney, pieced the two tracks together using Synclavier programming. The result is an affectionate blend of two of Bonzo's most illustrious moments.

LED ZEPPELIN REMASTERED 1993 BOXED SET II
ATLANTIC 82477

Good Times Bad Times / We're Gonna Groove / Night Flight / That's The Way / Baby Come On Home / The Lemon Song / You Shook Me / Boogie With Stu / Bron-Y-Aur / Down By The Seaside / Out On The Tiles / Black Mountain Side / Moby Dick / Sick Again / Hot Dog / Carouselambra / South Bound Suarez / Walter's Walk / Darlene / Black Country Woman / How Many More Times / The Rover / Four Sticks / Hats Off To (Roy) Harper / I Can't Quit You Baby / Hot's On For Nowhere / Livin' Lovin' Maid (She's Just A Woman) / Royal Orleans / Bonzo's Montreux / The Crunge / Bring It On Home / Tea For One

Due to the success of the first Remasters project, Jimmy Page responded to Atlantic's request that he work on the balance of tracks left off the set in readiness for a second box set release in 1993. After completing the mastering of the Coverdale/Page album at New York's Sterling Studios in the autumn of 1992,

Jimmy immediately set to work on the second Remasters set, again working with engineer George Marino.

The plan was to remaster the 31 performances from the Zeppelin catalogue that had been missed off the first compilation, and once again Jimmy gave careful consideration to the sequencing so as to again offer as balanced a

presentation as possible. Although most of the more familiar Zeppelin classics found their way on to the first box, this second collection incorporates many lesser acclaimed but equally important stepping stones. From the gentle acoustic beauty of 'That's The Way' and 'Bron-Y-Aur', through lengthy epics like 'How Many More Times' and 'Carouselambra' to off the wall nuggets like 'Walter's Walk' and 'Night Flight', the breadth of diversity is again quite startling and makes Boxed Set II a hugely enjoyable companion to the earlier collection.

And who knows... maybe the lack of any live material on this collection leaves the way open for Jimmy to one day produce that much touted and much requested official live chronological album for a Remasters III release.

Remasters II contains just one previously unissued track 'Baby Come On Home'...

BABY COME ON HOME
BURNS, PAGE, PLANT
STUDIO: OLYMPIC, LONDON

This track stems from an old master reel marked 'Yardbirds, October 10, 1968,' a clear reference to its vintage as being the period when the name Led Zeppelin was still under consideration. The master tape went mysteriously missing for a number of years and allegedly turned up in a refuse bin outside Olympic Studios in 1991.

On the original session the engineer dubs the track 'Tribute To Bert Berns', a reference to the renowned Sixties manager / producer / writer who wrote 'Twist And Shout' and 'Hang On Sloopy' and produced Van Morrison and Them amongst others. The original master tape of this first album outtake was dusted down and mixed by Mike Fraser, the co-producer of the Coverdale / Page album. Appearing now under the title Baby Come On Home, it's a welcome bonus, a slow blues tune and possibly Robert's idea carried over from The Band Of Joy. It's very commercial, with backing vocals on the chorus, Jones on Hammond organ and Jimmy confined to some low key Leslie guitar runs.

It's not hard to see why it didn't fit into the more energetic feel of the rest of the first album. Perhaps it was under consideration as an early single as it would have sat nicely alongside the '68 blues boom period releases from Fleetwood Mac, Chicken Shack and the like.

With every single Led Zeppelin studio recording remastered into a sequenced order for the Nineties by the man responsible for their original production, my advice is to line up the six CDs from the two sets, commence at 'Whole Lotta Love' on disc one, crank up the volume and wade through 86 performances aided by this guide to their catalogue and let the magic and memories of Led Zeppelin's music once again take you there...

NB: The original nine Led Zeppelin studio albums can also be found in remastered format packaged in the 1993 Atlantic box set 'Led Zeppelin – The Complete Studio Recordings' – catalogue number Atlantic 7825262.

Led Zeppelin at Knebworth, 1979

TRACK iNDEX

Achilles Last Stand 66
All My Love.................................82
Babe I'm Gonna Leave You 7
Baby Come On Home 100
Battle Of Evermore, The 35
Black Country Woman......................61
Black Dog...................................34
Black Mountain Side.........................9
Bonzo's Montreux 89
Boogie With Stu 60
Bring It On Home 21
Bron-Y-Aur 58
Bron-Y-Aur Stomp 29
Candy Store Rock 68
Carouselambra 82
Celebration Day.............................26
Communication Breakdown................10
Crunge, The.................................46
Custard Pie..................................53
Dancing Days 47

Darlene 88
Dazed And Confused 8, 73
Down By The Seaside 58
D'Yer Mak'er 47
Fool In The Rain 81
For Your Life 67
Four Sticks 38
Friends 25
Gallows Pole................................28
Going To California 38
Good Times Bad Times 5
Hats Off To Roy (Harper).................29
Heartbreaker................................18
Hey Hey What Can I Do 98
Hot Dog 81
Hots On For Nowhere 69
Houses Of the Holy 55
How Many More Times 11
I Can't Quit You Baby 10, 87
I'm Gonna Crawl 83

Immigrant Song 24
In My Time Of Dying 55
In The Evening 79
In The Light 57
Kashmir 56
Lemon Song, The 17
Livin' Lovin' Maid
   (She's Just A Woman) 18
Misty Mountain Hop 37
Moby Dick 20
Moby Dick/Bonzo's Montreux 75
Night Flight 59
No Quarter 48
Nobody's Fault But Mine 68
Ocean, The 49
Out On The Tiles 27
Over The Hills And Far Away 46
Ozone Baby 88
Poor Tom 87
Rain Song, The 45
Ramble On 20
Rock And Roll 34
Rover, The 54
Royal Orleans 67
Sick Again 61
Since I've Been Loving You 27
Song Remains The Same, The 44

South Bound Suarez 81
Stairway To Heaven 35, 74
Tangerine 28
Tea For One 69
Ten Years Gone 58
Thank You 17
That's The Way 28
Trampled Underfoot 56
Travelling Riverside Blues 97
Walter's Walk 88
Wanton Song, The 60
Wearing And Tearing 89
We're Gonna Groove 86
What Is And What Should Never Be .. 16
When The Levee Breaks 39
White Summer/Black Mountain Side . 98
Whole Lotta Love 14, 75
You Shook Me 7
Your Time Is Gonna Come 9

6/96 (24499)